"In *Meditation and Communion*, John Jeffe flection on the current malaise of the Weste and well-organized book. This is a wise and provocative book that revisits one of the most basic Christian acts—namely, the reading of Holy Scripture. Davis prophetically bridges the boundaries between descriptive analysis and constructive imagination. In the process, he returns to the church the gift of meditation, a word which for over a century has become identified mostly with non-Christian religions. If his challenge is taken seriously, we will never again read Scripture without an increasing sense of the presence of the risen Christ in our midst."

TIMOTHY C. TENNENT, professor of world Christianity
and president of Asbury Theological Seminary

"Finally, a book about meditation on Scripture that is theologically rich, built on the great Christian tradition, attuned to the contemporary scene and practically helpful! Jack Davis has provided a needed service to the church, one that will be spiritually refreshing to pastors, missionaries, teachers and laypeople alike. I for one was deeply challenged and encouraged by this fine book. I highly recommend it."

STEVE ROY, professor, Trinity Evangelical Divinity School,
and author, *What God Thinks When We Fail*

"Davis's passionate conviction that biblical meditation is an antidote to the bewildering busyness and fragmentation of twenty-first-century life shines through in this engaging, incisive work. Integrating theology and cutting-edge neuroscientific discovery, Davis creatively adapts meditative methods of the past for evangelicals in an age of technology, teaching us practical ways to grow deeply through our encounters with God's Word."

GWENFAIR WALTERS ADAMS, PH.D., associate professor of church history,
Gordon-Conwell Theological Seminary

"Jack Davis has taken key themes from contemporary theological study—inaugurated eschatology, union with Christ and communion with the Holy Trinity—and written about how they provide a fresh way to recover the ancient Christian practice of meditation upon Scripture. Biblically, theologically and historically learned as the author is, Davis sets his proposal in realistic discussions of popular culture, neuroscience and the widespread interest in Eastern meditation. This book leads the reader into the wonder and glory of a deeper life in God."

ANDREW PURVES, PH.D., professor of Reformed theology,
Pittsburgh Theological Seminary

"John Davis has written a much-needed book in this age of spiritual hunger and confusion. Working with insights from communication technology, recent discoveries of neuroscience and fresh understandings of the nature of the human person, Davis develops for us an engaging biblical and theological framework for authentic communion with the living God through meditating on the Scriptures. Focusing on the wonder of union with Christ, the good news of inaugurated eschatology and the unspeakable grace of sharing in the inner life of the Trinity, he opens up a fresh way to allow God to write the text into the hard-wire of our souls. What a gift!"

DARRELL JOHNSON, First Baptist Church, Vancouver

"John Jefferson Davis is one of the best and most important evangelical theologians alive today in North America. Whenever I read his works, I feel thrilled and fascinated by his profound insights and inspirations. *Meditation and Communion with God* is another superb example of his robust and thought-provoking theology. I enjoyed especially his engagement with other religious, primarily Asian, traditions. This book will be deeply loved by numerous readers not only in North America but also in the majority world. A must read for every Christian interested in biblical meditation, Trinitarian theology and symbolic hermeneutics."

SUNG WOOK CHUNG, associate professor of theology, Denver Seminary

MEDITATION
AND COMMUNION
WITH GOD

CONTEMPLATING SCRIPTURE
IN AN AGE OF DISTRACTION

JOHN JEFFERSON DAVIS

IVP Academic
An imprint of InterVarsity Press
Downers Grove, Illinois

InterVarsity Press
P.O. Box 1400, Downers Grove, IL 60515-1426
World Wide Web: www.ivpress.com
E-mail: email@ivpress.com

InterVarsity Press® is the book-publishing division of InterVarsity Christian Fellowship/USA®, a movement of
students and faculty active on campus at hundreds of universities, colleges and schools of nursing in the United States
of America, and a member movement of the International Fellowship of Evangelical Students. For information
about local and regional activities, write Public Relations Dept., InterVarsity Christian Fellowship/USA, 6400
Schroeder Rd., P.O. Box 7895, Madison, WI 53707-7895, or visit the IVCF website at <www.intervarsity.org>.

All Scripture quotations, unless otherwise indicated, are taken from the Holy Bible, New International Version®.
NIV®. Copyright ©1973, 1978, 1984 by International Bible Society. Used by permission of Zondervan Publishing
House. All rights reserved.

While all stories in this book are true, some names and identifying information in this book have been changed to
protect the privacy of the individuals involved.

Permission has been granted by the editor of Philosophia Christi to reprint "How Personal Agents Are Located in
Space," 13:2 (Summer 2011), 437-444. For more information about the journal, please visit epsociety.org.

Cover design: Cindy Kiple
Interior design: Beth Hagenberg
Images: © ChrisAt/iStockphoto

ISBN 978-0-8308-3976-6

Printed in the United States of America ∞

Library of Congress Cataloging-in-Publication Data has been requested.

P	20	19	18	17	16	15	14	13	12	11	10	9	8	7	6	5	4
Y	29	28	27	26	25	24	23	22	21	20	19	18					

Contents

1

INTRODUCTION

Reality in Meditation

〰
〰

Wнy ANOTHER BOOK ON MEDITATION NOW? This book on
Christian and biblical meditation grows out of my own personal experience with meditation. A number of years ago, when my family and I
were facing some times of turbulence and stress, I was drawn—providentially, I believe—to an extended time of meditation on the first chapter
of Paul's letter to the Ephesians. Morning after morning, for about a
six-month period, I slowly and prayerfully, without any particular agenda,
reflected on the words and verses of this great exposition of God's eternal
purposes for his people, rooted in eternity past and reaching into eternity
future. This time of reflection, linking the truths of Ephesians to other
texts in the biblical canon, was my own discovery of the spiritually satisfying and ancient practice of biblical meditation, though I was not really
familiar with the history of this ancient Christian practice at the time.
This six-month period of sustained meditation on this biblical text was
one of the most—indeed, perhaps the most—spiritually transformative
experience of my own Christian pilgrimage. New insights into the
meaning of life in Christ, of God's plan for his people, and as significantly, a quiet but very real sense of being directly in the presence of God,
came out of this very special time. Now, years later, I wish to bolster this
spiritually transformative experience of biblical meditation with subsequent research in biblical and systematic theology, our contemporary cul-

tural context, comparative religion, and cognitive sciences and neurosciences, with a view to sharing these insights with pastors, seminarians and all those who are followers of Jesus and interested in a deeper and more reflective encounter with God through the holy Scriptures.

Beyond my own personal experience, I see at least six factors today that would seem to make a fresh investigation of the theological roots of biblical meditation a timely project for the contemporary church. First, the renewal of interest in the spiritual disciplines in evangelical Protestant circles in the last generation, and especially since the publication of Richard Foster's seminal book of 1978, *Celebration of Discipline*. Second, the growing religious pluralism of American culture and the growing interest in Asian religions and Buddhist and Hindu meditation practices. Third, the secularization of American culture and concerns for biblical illiteracy in society and the churches. Fourth, growing awareness and concern about the impact of the Internet and digital media on reading habits, the ability to concentrate and to focus the mind, and on levels of personal distraction and stress. Fifth, new scientific research in the fields of neuroscience and cognitive science that have studied the effects of meditation on the brain and personal health. Sixth, trends in biblical and systematic theology, including the renewal of interest in trinitarian theology and union with Christ, that have yet to be systematically integrated into a theology supporting ancient Christian practices such as meditating on Scripture.

I write this book out of a firm conviction that the practice of biblical meditation can be an invaluable source of spiritual growth and renewal for any Christian, and that such practices are especially vital for pastors, priests, seminarians, missionaries, teachers and other Christian workers who constantly face the challenges of stress, burnout and spiritual dryness in the midst of the demands of ministry.

The plan of this book is as follows: first, I will survey the larger cultural context in which the Bible is read, examining the six factors noted above; second, I will propose a new understanding of the nature and practice of biblical meditation as *communion with God* who is *really present* to the reader—based on a biblical and theological framework focusing on the doctrines of union with Christ and inaugurated eschatology. In the course of this discussion I will also be arguing for a rehabilitation of the ancient fourfold sense of Scripture (*literal* or historical-grammatical sense, *moral* or ethical sense, *tropological* or christological sense, and the *anagogical* or heavenly sense), understood in relation to the New Testament teachings concerning the believer's union with Christ and the "already" aspects of the kingdom of God inaugurated with the death, resurrection and ascension of Christ, and the coming of the Holy Spirit: the kingdom of God has *already* begun to arrive, and the risen Jesus is present with his people in the Spirit.

In connection with this proposed retrieval of the ancient and patristic fourfold sense of Scripture, I will also argue for a fresh understanding in evangelical Protestant circles of the notions of *metaphor*, *symbol* and *imagination*. In the course of this argument I will be drawing from modern research in the cognitive sciences and neurosciences that provides support for what I will propose as a whole-brain method of biblical meditation, integrating both words and images. I will also be presenting arguments based on concepts and analogies drawn from the Internet and digital media that provide new ways of conceptualizing how God is really present to the believing community in worship and in the devotional reading of Scripture.

In the third and final section of this book I will present the practical applications of the previous theological framework, outlining actual meditation practices at three different levels of proficiency: first, a simple, introductory method of biblical meditation focused on a single biblical text; second, an intermediate-level method of whole-brain meditation, linking two or more texts on a biblical theme, bringing together both concepts and images; and third, a more advanced method of worldview meditation: the "five practices of right comprehension," a method of meditation that encompasses the essentials of a comprehensive *Christian worldview* that can reinforce the practices of both the introductory and intermediate-level methods. This section on practice will provide practical suggestions on how to meditate and illustrations with specific biblical texts and passages. The bibliography and appendixes will provide further resources for those who wish to deepen their understanding and practice of biblical meditation.

2

READING SCRIPTURE TODAY

Communion with God in an Age of Distraction

∿∿
∿∿

A RENAISSANCE OF INTEREST IN THE SPIRITUAL DISCIPLINES

The publication of Richard Foster's *Celebration of Discipline* (1978) and of Dallas Willard's *The Spirit of the Disciplines* (1988) sparked a renewal of interest in spiritual disciplines in evangelical circles that has continued unabated to the present day.[1] This renewal of interest in the spiritual disciplines in Protestant circles can be seen in the context of an earlier renewal of interest in Scripture study and classic practices such as the meditative reading of Scripture in Roman Catholicism encouraged by the Second Vatican Council (1962-1965). In the "Dogmatic Constitution on Divine Revelation" the council "earnestly and specifically" urged "all the Christian faithful, too, especially the religious, to learn by frequent reading of the divine Scriptures the 'excelling knowledge of Jesus Christ' (Phil 3:8). 'For ignorance of the

---

[1]Richard J. Foster, *Celebration of Discipline: The Path to Spiritual Growth* (New York: Harper & Row, 1978); Dallas Willard, *The Spirit of the Disciplines: Understanding How God Changes Lives* (New York: HarperCollins, 1988). In 1989 Willard founded the Renovaré Institute for Christian Spiritual Formation, out of a concern that, in his view, at present "the spiritual formation field lacks intellectual rigor and testable information needed to put the gospel and spiritual life in Christ on the cognitive map for the multitudes of people who are hungry for something real" (Dallas Willard, "Renovaré: Vision and Mission Statement," Dallas Willard.org, www.dwillard.org/calendar/Renovare_Institute.pdf).

Scriptures is ignorance of Christ.'"[2] The ancient monastic practice of a prayerful, meditative reading of Scripture that had been languishing a bit in the modern period was newly energized in monastic and scholarly Roman Catholic circles by the council's encouragement.[3]

The renewal of interest in more contemplative forms of spirituality in evangelical circles reflected a growing sense that the more activistic elements of the tradition—preaching, programs, meetings—were still leaving many pastors and laypeople less than fully nourished spiritually. Many resonated with the observations of Peter Scazzero, a busy and successful pastor of New Life Fellowship, a large multiracial church in Queens, New York. Too many Christians today, he noted, feel "overscheduled, tense, frantic, preoccupied, fatigued, and starved for time. . . . We are too active for the kind of reflection needed to sustain a life of love with God and others."[4]

Other thoughtful evangelical leaders were increasingly realizing that spiritual disciplines such as meditation on Scripture were essential for the lasting personal growth and spiritual transformation that many were desiring but not experiencing. "We evangelicals are deeply committed to the Gospel, evangelism, and missions. Rumor has it, however, that spiritual hunger is endemic in the church," observed Bruce Demarest, professor of Christian formation at Denver Seminary. "The evangelical church has not been suffering from a lack of effort," according to Demarest, "but our regimens of sanctification may be too

---

[2]"Dogmatic Constitution on Divine Revelation," in *The Documents of Vatican II*, ed. Walter M. Abbott (New York: Corpus Books, 1966), p. 127.

[3]In the patristic and Catholic tradition, such a meditative reading of Scripture was called *lectio divina* (a "spiritual" way of reading). See, for example, the following publications since the 1970s by Catholic scholars: Susan Muto, *A Practical Guide to Spiritual Reading* (Danville, N.J.: Dimension, 1976); Thelma Hall, *Too Deep for Words* (Mahwah, N.J.: Paulist Press, 1988); Michael Casey, *Sacred Reading: The Ancient Art of Lectio Divina* (Ligouri, Mo.: Triumph Books, 1996); Mariono Magrassi, *Praying the Bible: An Introduction to Lectio Divina* (Collegeville, Minn.: Liturgical Press, 1998); Basil M. Pennington, *Lectio Divina: Renewing the Ancient Practice of Praying the Scriptures* (New York: Crossroad, 1998); and Enzo Bianchi, *Praying the Word: an Introduction to Lectio Divina* (Kalamazoo, Mich.: Cistercian Studies, 1999).

[4]Peter Scazzero, *Emotionally Healthy Spirituality* (Nashville: Thomas Nelson, 2006), p. 48. Scazzero, at one point near burnout in his own ministry, decided to adopt a more contemplative spirituality: "Being productive and getting things done are high priorities in our Western culture. Praying and enjoying God's presence for no other reason than to delight in him was a luxury, I was told, that we could take pleasure in once we got to heaven. For now, there was too much to be done" (ibid., p. 31).

programmatic, activist, and fast. We engage in considerable religious activity with uncertain levels of transformation."[5]

Seminary students at times find that the academic study of the Bible and the time demands of graduate theological education leave them spiritually dry and frustrated. One student at an evangelical seminary in the United States stated in an interview that at times the seminary's

> emphasis on academic excellence . . . creates a campus climate where attaining spiritual depth is difficult. . . . Professors encourage students to have an intimate relationship with God, but the amount of work assigned is so great and the other commitments required of students are so numerous, this becomes a virtual impossibility. . . . I get the sense that many of my fellow students are going into ministry equipped to parse, translate, and exegete, but spiritually dead or distant from the God who speaks in and through the text.[6]

In a recent extensive internal study the leadership of the influential Willow Creek Community Church in South Barrington, Illinois, found to its surprise that significant numbers of their most active members and attendees reported feeling stalled in their spiritual lives, despite the rich and diverse menu of programs and activities at the church. "We were not prepared to discover that so many people are stalled in their spiritual lives, and certainly not prepared to find that some of our best disciples were among those most dissatisfied with the church," stated the lead authors of the *Reveal* self-study. "We were also surprised that personal spiritual practices played such a critical role—showing up as the primary catalyst for growth in the most advanced spiritual segments."[7] The Willow Creek leadership team concluded that "Our people need to learn to feed themselves through personal spiritual practices that allow them to deepen their relationship to Christ."[8]

A younger generation of evangelical Christians who are increasingly committed to ministries of social justice are also realizing that

[5]Bruce Demarest, "Spiritual Formation: Fleeting Fad or Return to Roots?" *Denver Seminary Magazine* 2, no. 2 (2006): 10.
[6]"Student Responses to 2008 Strategic Planning Survey," unpublished document, pp. 22-23.
[7]Greg L. Hawkins and Cally Parkinson, *Reveal: Where Are You? The Brutal Truth About Spiritual Growth* (Barrington, Ill.: Willow Creek Association, 2007), p. 58.
[8]Ibid., p. 65.

to sustain such commitments inner spiritual depth and staying power are needed. "Our experience with social justice has led us to see," noted Evan Howard, "that outer change without inner change has little staying power and often leads to burnout for those devoting themselves to kingdom work. We are ready for a good dose of inner spiritual transformation."[9]

The need for more effective means of personal spiritual transformation has also been highlighted by evangelical advocates of social justice such as Ron Sider. In *The Scandal of the Evangelical Conscience* Sider noted that standards of personal behavior by many self-identified evangelical Christians in America do not seem to be very different from that of non-Christians. White evangelicals are the people who are *most* likely to object to neighbors of another race; evangelical youth differ little from their peers in areas such as premarital sexual activity; divorce rates are higher in the southern United States, where conservative Protestants make up a higher percentage of the population than elsewhere in the country; a large study by the Christian Reformed Church found that physical and sexual abuse were as common as in the general population.[10] Such findings would appear to support the conclusion that attending church and hearing good sermons, while certainly of great value, do not in themselves lead to the deeper encounters with God through the Scriptures that produce lasting personal transformation.

RELIGIOUS PLURALISM IN AMERICA
THE SALAD BAR OF SPIRITUAL PRACTICES

A formerly "Christian America" that could be described in terms of "Protestant, Catholic, Jew" can now be described as "the world's most religiously diverse nation."[11] In 1965 President Lyndon Johnson signed

---

[9]Evan Howard, "Three Temptations of Spiritual Formation," *Christianity Today*, December 9, 2002, p. 1, www.christianitytoday.com/ct/2002/december9/4.46.html. Howard is director of the Spirituality Shoppe, an evangelical center for the study of Christian spirituality in Montrose, Colorado, and the author of *Praying the Scriptures* (Downers Grove, Ill.: InterVarsity Press, 1999).

[10]Ronald J. Sider, *The Scandal of the Evangelical Conscience: Why Are Christians Living Just Like the Rest of the World?* (Grand Rapids: Baker, 2005), pp. 13, 19, 27.

[11]"Protestant, Catholic, Jew" is an allusion to the influential book by Will Herberg originally published in 1956, *Protestant, Catholic, Jew: An Essay in American Religious Sociology* (Garden

into law the Immigration and Naturalization Act, opening America's doors to immigrants from Asia, who had been excluded since 1924.[12] Linked in spirit to the Civil Rights Act, which had been passed the year before, this action brought waves of immigrants from Southeast Asia, India, Korea, China and Japan—and with them the Buddhist, Hindu and other Eastern religions and practices of their countries of origin. Americans, during the socially turbulent 1960s, could now choose from a tantalizing and exotic menu of Eastern meditative practices that heretofore had been primarily known only to a scholarly elite. More than ever, it would seem, Christians who are interested in cultivating spiritual depth and new spiritual practices need some guidance on *which* forms of spirituality to pursue and some help in rediscovering a classic spiritual practice—meditating on Scripture—that is in fact an important but neglected part of their own Protestant heritage.

Eastern meditation arrived on America's shores most visibly in the forms of Transcendental Meditation, yoga and various Buddhist traditions—Zen, Theravada and Tibetan.[13] While in absolute numbers and percentage of the North American population, both Buddhism and Hinduism are relatively small (Buddhists: 1.1 percent; Hindus: .5 percent),[14] both of these Eastern religious traditions have had impacts far beyond what these small numbers would suggest, due in part to the facts that Buddhists and Hindus in the United States tend to be more highly educated and more affluent than the general population, concentrated in the urban areas and centers of cultural influence, and represent exotic alter-

---

City, N.J.: Doubleday, 1956), in which these three religious preferences were, at the time, fairly accurate descriptors of the American religious landscape. The latter phrase is drawn from the subtitle of the book by Diana L. Eck, *A New Religious America: How a "Christian Country" Has Become the World's Most Religiously Diverse Nation* (New York: HarperCollins, 2001). Eck is professor of comparative religion at Harvard and director of the Harvard Pluralism Project.

[12]Ibid., p. 6. Immigration from China had been prohibited since 1882.

[13]Although the focus in this section is on Hindu and Buddhist forms of meditation, practices rooted in Islam (Sufism) and Judaism are also present in the American religious scene. For Sufi meditative practices see Daniel Goleman, *The Meditative Mind: The Varieties of Meditative Experience* (Los Angeles: Jeremy P. Tarcher, 1988), pp. 59-66; on the renewed interest in meditation among American Jews, see Nan Fink Gefen, *Discovering Jewish Meditation: Instruction and Guidance For Learning an Ancient Spiritual Practice* (Woodstock, Vt.: Jewish Lights, 1999).

[14]Todd M. Johnson and Kenneth R. Ross, eds., *Atlas of Global Christianity: 1910-2010* (Edinburgh: Edinburgh University Press, 2009), pp. 13, 15.

natives to Christianity that many spiritual seekers find attractive.[15]

Transcendental Meditation (TM) was introduced to the West during the late 1950s by Maharishi Mahesh Yogi, an Indian guru trained in the *Advaita Vedanta* or monistic stream of Hinduism. His teachings in the United States attracted increasing attention during the 1960s, especially after celebrities such as the Beatles, Mia Farrow and Jane Fonda were trained in his meditative techniques.[16] Presented as a technique, like speed reading, that could help the practitioner achieve stress reduction, concentration and health benefits, TM had been introduced to about one million Americans by 1975.[17] The Maharishi went on to establish Maharishi International University in Iowa in 1974 to propagate his teachings and practices, and by the end of the century had established centers in 108 countries and had trained some six million people in his basic meditation courses.[18]

All the major Buddhist traditions—Theravada, Zen, Tibetan—and their meditation practices are represented in America. Within an hour's drive from downtown Washington, D.C., one can find Buddhist temples and monks from Thailand, Vietnam, Japan, Korea, Sri Lanka and Tibet.[19] In any large bookstore such as Barnes and Noble, one is likely to find more titles on the shelves by the Dalai Lama than by Billy Graham or Pope Benedict. Since receiving the Noble Peace Prize in 1989, the Dalai Lama (Tenzin Gyatso), the leader of Tibetan Buddhism, has become something of a "religious rock star" in America, spreading the dharma on college campuses and universities and maintaining a high and favorable profile in the media. Tibetan Buddhist

---

[15]According to one recent study of American religious demographics, nearly three out of four Americans who identify themselves as Buddhist are converts to Buddhism—rather than immigrants from Asia who brought their religion with them ("Religion in America," Pew Forum on Religion & Public Life [2010], http://religions.pewforum.org/reports).

[16]Kim Knott, "Transcendental Meditation," in *Encyclopedia of New Religious Movements*, ed. Peter B. Clarke (London: Routledge, 2006), p. 573.

[17]Gene R. Thursby, "Hindu Movements Since Mid-Century: Yogis in the United States," in *America's Alternative Religions*, ed. Timothy Miller (Albany: State University of New York Press, 1995), pp. 194-95.

[18]Ibid., p. 195; Knott, "Transcendental Meditation," p. 573.

[19]Jane Hurst, "Buddhism in America: The Dharma in the Land of the Red Man," in *America's Alternative Religions*, ed. Timothy Miller (Albany: State University of New York Press, 1995), pp. 161.

meditation practices are taught at study centers such as the Nyingma Institute in Berkeley, California, and the even larger school in Boulder, Colorado, the Naropa Institute. Buddhist publishing houses such as Shambhala Press, Wisdom Publications and Dharma Publishing are furnishing a growing stream of books on Buddhist thought and meditation for the American religious market.[20]

Diana Eck has observed that there are now at least four Buddhist meditation centers within a five-mile radius of Harvard Square in Cambridge, Massachusetts. Of the hundreds of seekers who frequent these centers, some would call themselves Buddhists, but many are likely to be from some Christian background—Methodist, Catholic, Episcopalian. "This serious 'crossing over' into the spiritual terrain of an Eastern religious tradition," Eck notes, "is one of the most important spiritual movements of today." According to Eck, a leading scholar of religious pluralism, Buddhist meditation "is becoming an important strand of Christian spirituality."[21] This so-called phenomenon of "crossing over"—Christians adopting Buddhist and other religions' spiritual practices—can be a symptom of ignorance of one's own spiritual heritage and a further reason to retrieve a *Christian* and *biblical* theology and practice of meditation.

As part of her research Eck has interviewed Roman Catholic teachers such as William Johnston, Anthony de Mello and John Main, who have brought Buddhist and Hindu practices into their own practices of Christian prayer and meditation.[22] The Vatican's Congregation for the Doctrine of the Faith, in a pastoral letter, "Letter to the Bishops of the

---

[20]Ibid., pp. 168-69.

[21]Diana L. Eck, *Encountering God: A Spiritual Journey from Bozeman to Banaras* (Boston: Beacon Press, 1993), p. 153.

[22]Ibid., pp. 159-60. See William Johnston, *The Still Point: Reflections on Zen and Christian Mysticism* (New York: Fordham University Press, 1970); Anthony de Mello, *Sadhana: A Way to God* (St. Louis: Institute of Jesuit Sources, 1979); John Main, *The Present Christ: Further Steps in Meditation* (London: Darton, Longman & Todd, 1985); see also Kemens Tilmann, *The Practice of Meditation* (New York: Paulist Press, 1977): "a variety of methods . . . from the Eastern and Western traditions." More recently, the book by the Roman Catholic scholar Paul Knitter, a prominent voice in interreligious studies, *Without Buddha I Could Not Be a Christian* (Oxford: OneWorld, 2009), represents Knitter's attempt to "cross over" into Buddhism while still remaining a Catholic Christian. Knitter, whose wife is a Buddhist, is Paul Tillich Professor of Theology, World Religions and Culture at Union Theological Seminary in New York City.

Catholic Church on Some Aspects of Christian Meditation," cautioned Roman Catholics to avoid the dangers of spiritual syncretism that could attend an uncritical appropriation of Eastern meditation practices.[23]

At this point a Christian reader of this book—especially, perhaps, an evangelical Protestant reader—may be wondering, *Must I "go East" in order to learn how to meditate? This only increases my suspicion of the whole business of "meditation."* The question is a fair one. Over thirty years ago the Christian psychologist Paul Vitz made the following observations about the American religious landscape, and his observations seem if anything more timely than ever:

> The search for transcendence . . . is now firmly begun. Browse in any bookstore. . . . Here are the books on Buddhism, the Tao, *I Ching*, Transcendental Meditation, altered states of consciousness, Yoga, and so on. We are all aware of the Eastern religious revival. The country is full of holy men—Sri Chinmoy, Maharishi, Yogi Gupta, Baba Ram Dass. . . . But where are the Christian holy ones? Where are the Christian mystical messengers to our pagan universities and suburbs?[24]

Indeed, where are the Christian "holy ones"? This book is written in the conviction that the Christian tradition has its own very rich heritage of meditative and contemplative practice, and that this heritage should be freshly discovered and appreciated by many Christians today.

Evangelical Christians are understandably wary of uncritically adopting Eastern religious practices, but as Simon Chan has reminded us, evangelical Protestantism has its own rich heritage of biblical meditation, and this heritage needs to be retrieved and adapted to today's spiritual needs.[25] Over forty Puritan authors and their successors in the

---

[23]"Letter to the Bishops of the Catholic Church on Some Aspects of Christian Meditation," Congregation of the Doctrine of the Faith, October 15, 1989, www.ewtn.com/library/curia/cdfmed.htm. The letter was signed by then Joseph Cardinal Ratzinger, now Benedict XVI.

[24]Paul C. Vitz, *Psychology as Religion: The Cult of Self-Worship* (Grand Rapids: Eerdmans, 1977), p. 134.

[25]Simon Chan, *Spiritual Theology: A Systematic Study of the Christian Life* (Downers Grove, Ill.: InterVarsity Press, 1998). Chan states his belief that [Western] evangelicalism, with its somewhat " rational approach to Scripture and its negative attitude toward non-Western culture has either explicitly or implicitly discouraged the use of the meditative approach to Scripture" (ibid., p. 171). Chan, a Chinese evangelical theologian teaching at Trinity Theological College in Singapore, wrote his doctoral dissertation at Cambridge on the topic "The Puritan Meditative Tradition, 1599-1691: A Study in Ascetical Piety."

Puritan and Reformed tradition wrote treatises and sermons on biblical meditation, among which could be mentioned the following: Thomas Boston, *Duty and Advantage of Solemn Meditation*; William Bridge, *The Work and Way of Meditation*; William Bates, *On Divine Meditation*; Thomas Manton, *[Ten] Sermons Upon Genesis 24:63* ("Isaac went out to the field one evening to meditate"); Thomas Watson, *A Christian on the Mount; or, a Treatise Concerning Meditation*; Robert L. Dabney, *Meditation as a Means of Grace*; William G. T. Shedd, *Religious Meditation*, in *Sermons to the Spiritual Man*.[26]

According to Joel Beeke, a Netherlands Reformed minister in Grand Rapids and student of the Puritans, for the Puritans, meditation was a solemn obligation and *duty* for every serious Christian: "One cannot be a Christian without meditation," in the Puritan view. Without meditation, "Preaching won't benefit us, our prayers won't be effective, and we will be unable to defend the truth." For them, meditation was the duty that gave rise to all other Christian duties and "lubricated" all the other means of grace.[27]

Meditation and Communion with God seeks, from an explicitly biblical and Christian point of view, to promote a form of Christian meditation based on a robust biblical and *Christian* theology, and informed by insights from recent scientific research and interreligious studies, where such insights are consistent with the core teachings of the Christian faith.

BIBLICAL ILLITERACY IN AMERICA

Pastor David Platt's fifty-five-minute Sunday sermons at the Church at Brook Hills in Birmingham, Alabama, are, needless to say, much longer than the typical sermon in American churches. During his travels Platt was deeply impressed by Chinese underground house church Bible study sessions that, under threat of persecution, could last as long as twelve hours at a single sitting.[28] Inspired by this example,

---

[26]Full citations to these Puritan and Reformed authors are found in Robert P. Martin, *A Guide to the Puritans* (Edinburgh: Banner of Truth, 1997), p. 157.

[27]Joel Beeke, "The Puritan Practice of Meditation," in *Wherein Consists Reformed Spirituality?* Greenville Seminary Theology Conference on "Communing with Our Glorious God," March 12-14, 2002, www.banneroftruth.org/pages/articles/article_detail.php?119.

[28]Collin Hansen, "Why Johnny Can't Read the Bible," *Christianity Today*, May 24, 2010, p. 1,

Platt started "Secret Church" meetings at his church starting at 6 p.m., preaching on a single topic such as the atonement or Old Testament survey until midnight; such events have become so popular that Platt has had to require advance tickets for admission.[29]

In the culture at large, however, much anecdotal evidence indicates that biblical illiteracy is pervasive in the United States today. The reality of biblical illiteracy—in a nation awash in Bibles—is yet another reason that American Christians should be rediscovering the ancient, time-tested ways of spending *more* time with Scripture, rather than less.

A cover story in *Time* magazine in 2007 reported that only about one-half of U.S. adults could name *one* of the four Gospels, and that fewer than half could identify Genesis as the first book of the Bible.[30] More careful studies by the Barna Research Group have given credibility to such concerns. In a year-in-review study conducted in 2009, the Barna researchers discovered that most Americans, by the time they reach the age of thirteen or fourteen, believe that they know much of what the Bible has to teach and have little further interest in learning more biblical content.[31] The Barna studies have also documented a pervasive *eclecticism* and *individualism* in the way many Americans read the Bible. "The Christian faith is less a life perspective that challenges the supremacy of individualism as it is a faith being defined through individualism," the researchers concluded.[32] Many Americans are prone to a "cut-and-paste" spirituality, embracing an "unpredictable and contradictory body of beliefs," with "feelings and emotions . . . more significant than information-based exercises such as listening to preaching and participating in Bible study."[33]

While studies of biblical literacy in the general population are of interest, more to the point for readers of this book are questions such as

---

www.christianitytoday.com/ct/2010/may/25.38.html.

[29]Ibid., p. 3.

[30]Ibid., p. 1.

[31]"Year-in-Review Perspective" (2009), Barna Research Group, www.barna.org/barna-update/article/12-faithspirituality/325-barna-studies, "Theme 3."

[32]"Christianity Is No Longer American's Default Faith," Barna Group, January 12, 2009, www.barna.org/barna-update/article/12-faithspirituality/15.

[33]Ibid.

How much time do *Christians* in America spend reading the Bible? Light has been shed on this significant question by the study "Biblical Literacy and Spiritual Growth: Survey Results," conducted by the Center for Biblical Engagement in Lincoln, Nebraska.[34] This study, based on 8,665 respondents across the United States, of which 99.7 percent were self-identified "followers of Jesus Christ" (and 75 percent identifying as followers for ten or more years), found that 85 percent of the respondents said they read the Bible more than once a week; about one-half reported reading the Bible for thirty minutes per session, but only one in ten reported reading the Bible for more than thirty minutes in a session. The study found that those who read the Bible at least four times a week were less likely to engage in behaviors such as gambling, pornography, alcohol abuse, and sex outside of marriage. The researchers also concluded that "time spent in the Word correlates with an individual's spiritual growth, including his or her knowledge of the Bible and attempts to share his or her faith."[35]

When the survey respondents were asked why they did not spend more time reading the Bible, the most common response was that they were too busy. In connection with this sense of the rushed nature of modern American life, an item in a recent Zondervan ChurchSource catalog caught my attention: an advertisement for the *Busy Dad's Bible: Daily Inspiration Even If You Only Have One Minute.* The ad assured the reader that this Bible for busy dads, packed with "one-minute thought starters" could be the "perfect support for the time-starved dad who longs to connect with God to find wisdom and encouragement."[36] I sincerely hope that busy dads who use this Bible do indeed find at least one minute's spiritual nourishment—but I hope even more in this book to promote a more reflective and leisurely engagement with Scripture in real meditation! The data just cited in the Center for Biblical En-

---

[34]The figures cited here are from the study "Biblical Literacy & Spiritual Growth: Survey Results, November 2006," available at www.centerforbibleengagement.org/images/stories/pdf/cbe_survey_results.pdf.

[35]Ibid., p. iv.

[36]Busy moms are not being forgotten; the *New Mom's Prayer Bible*, with fifty-two "one minute Thought Starters," also has an option for a "five-minute prayer or ten-minute study to help you learn even more about what God's Word has to say to you today": ChurchSource fall catalog 2010, p. 19.

gagement survey is consistent with the conclusion that the practice of biblical meditation contributes significantly to a Christian's spiritual growth and is more likely to lead to personal transformation than more superficial forms of engagement with the Bible.

READING THE BIBLE IN AN AGE OF INFORMATION OVERLOAD

Kord Campbell, a California software entrepreneur, goes to sleep with his laptop or iPhone on his chest, and goes online shortly after waking up. Then he works from his office with two computer screens buzzing with emails, instant messages, online chats, an active Web browser and files of computer code that he is writing.[37] His wife Brenda says that Kord at times forgets dinner plans, craves the stimulation that he gets from his digital gadgets and struggles with focusing on his family. According to Brenda, "It seems like he can no longer be fully in the moment."[38]

Kord and Brenda's situation is not that unusual in a culture struggling with the challenges of information overload. Recent studies have indicated that already by 2008, Americans were consuming three times as much information each day as they did in 1960.[39] The amount of data generated by the Internet, computers, research labs, sensors, cameras and phones has been growing at a compound rate of 60 percent annually, and as of 2008, American households were being bombarded with thirty-four gigabytes of information per person per day, the biggest "information hogs" being video games and television.[40]

In a recent five-year period there has been an enormous increase in media use among young people, with the average adolescent spending over seven and a half hours each day, seven days a week, consuming various forms of media.[41] When multitasking is taken into account, these youths actually pack ten hours and forty-five minutes of media

[37]Matt Richtel, "Attached to Technology and Paying a Price," *New York Times*, June 6, 2010, www.nytimes.com/2010/06/07/technology/07brain.html.
[38]Ibid.
[39]Ibid., p. 3.
[40]"All Too Much: Monstrous Amounts of Data," *Economist*, February 27, 2010, p. 5.
[41]"Generation M²: Media in the Lives of 8- to 18-Year Olds: Key Findings," *Kaiser Family Foundation Study*, January 2010, p. 1.

use into those seven and a half hours. Every type of media use *except* reading has increased in the last ten years.[42]

This enormous explosion in the sheer *quantity* of information we are exposed to in the modern world is having important *qualitative* effects on our health and relationships, on how we read, learn and pay attention, and even how we construct and nurture our sense of personal identity. Information overload also has crucial implications for how we read the Bible and makes a slow, unhurried and reflective reading of Scripture more vital than ever.

Modern information technology makes our lives easier in some ways and vastly increases our access to information, but also can increase our levels of stress with the relentless flow of messages that distract us, interrupt us and call for immediate attention. One recent study found that the typical computer user at work checks email or changes windows or other programs nearly thirty-seven times each hour.[43] Such constant interruptions take their psychic toll. Careful studies of multitasking are now showing that such fragmented attention impedes learning and long-term retention of information.[44]

The Internet and other digital technologies are now changing the way many people read. Nicholas Carr has cited research that shows that Web pages are typically skimmed, not read from start to finish, in an "F" pattern that scans the first two lines and then zips down the page, looking for snippets of useful information.[45] The online environment, according to Carr, is one that "promotes cursory reading, hurried and distracted thinking, and superficial learning."[46] Carr's concerns are not unduly alarmist but are in fact supported by a significant body of research. After an extensive review of the research

---

[42]Ibid.

[43]Richtel, "Attached to Technology and Paying a Price," p. 2.

[44]Patricia Greenfield, "Technology and Informal Education: What Is Taught, What Is Learned," *Science* 23 (2009): 70. "Distracting information exacts a cognitive cost, even from the younger generation who have had more experience with multitasking. A controlled experiment showed that college students recalled significantly fewer facts from four main news stories in CNN's visually complex environment than from the same stories presented in a visually simple format, with the news anchor alone on the screen and the news crawls etc. edited out" (ibid.).

[45]Nicholas Carr, *The Shallows: What the Internet Is Doing to Our Brains* (New York: W. W. Norton), p. 134.

[46]Ibid., p. 116.

literature, educational psychologist Patricia Greenfield concluded that while the Internet and video games can enhance certain forms of "visual intelligence," the cognitive cost is high: "The cost seems to be deep processing: mindful knowledge acquisition, inductive analysis, critical thinking, imagination, and reflection"—exactly the types of cognitive skills that are increasingly important in today's complex, information-rich world.[47]

The Internet and social media such as Facebook and Twitter can be not only sources of distraction and time consumption, but can subtly affect the shaping of our personal identities and character. Sherry Turkle, an MIT professor, interviewed some four hundred children and parents to document their cell phone and social media usage for her book *Alone Together*.[48] She discovered that among many of these young people the sense of self was increasingly

> becoming externally manufactured rather than internally developed . . . because you're . . . creating something for others' consumption, you find yourself imagining and playing to your audience more and more. So those moments in which you're supposed to be showing your true self become a performance.[49]

On the other hand, in moments of reflective and prayerful meditation on Scripture, we can be ourselves in the presence of the One who truly knows us, before whom we do not need to perform, and who seeks communion with us in a "friend" relationship deeper than Facebook can provide. Meditation can provide a much needed island of authenticity in the midst of the ocean of digital media.

The challenge of dealing with information overload in an Internet age is a very visible manifestation of a larger cultural problem: the *rushed nature* of modern life and a cult of speed, efficiency and production. "Today we are addicted to speed, to cramming more and more into every minute," notes Carl Honore, author of the bestselling book *In Praise of*

[47]Greenfield, "Technology and Informal Education," p. 71.
[48]Peggy Orenstein, "I Tweet, Therefore I Am," *New York Times*, July 30, 2010, www.nytimes.com/2010/08/01/magazine/01wwln-lede-t.html.
[49]Ibid.

Slow.[50] "This roadrunner culture," he says, "is taking a toll on everything from our health, diet and work to our communities, relationships and the environment."[51] The "Slow Movement," which began in Italy in the 1990s as a reaction to fast food, is an attempt to push back against the cult of speed and has spawned daughter movements such as Slow Travel, Slow Dating and Slow Reading. John Miedema, author of *Slow Reading*, has pointed out the obvious: "Our attention can only manage so many stimuli. With the endless stream of information fed to us in modern life, our attention is compromised . . . The web . . . displaces time and attention we might spend really savoring a good read."[52] Digital technologies and the Internet are not themselves the root of the problem, he argues; the real problems "are our weakness for speed and attempts to attend to too many things at once. We cannot accelerate our lives indefinitely. At some point we have to slow down to get a handle on our information."[53]

The historic Christian practice of meditating on Scripture is, of course, just such an example of "slow reading." In the face of today's rushed lives and information overload, such slow reading of the Word of God seems more important than ever. Some texts we may skim for information, other texts we may browse for entertainment, but in our meditation on Scripture, we are seeking *communion and friendship with God* for its own sake and for the sake of our souls. What is being encouraged in this book is not avoidance of digital and Internet technologies—an impossible and counterproductive stance—but rather a more reflective and intentional use of them, and a slower, more contemplative reading of Scripture. As Wen Stephenson, formerly an editor for the *Atlantic Monthly*, has noted, today's media environment requires a "new kind of self-discipline, a willed and practiced ability to focus, in a purposeful and almost meditative sense—to step away from the network and seek stillness, immersion."[54] The discipline of meditating on Scripture can develop

---

[50]Carl Honore, *In Praise of Slow: How A Worldwide Movement Is Challenging the Cult of Speed* (Toronto: Alfred A. Knopf, 2004); see www.carlhonore.com/?page_id=6.
[51]Ibid.
[52]John Miedema, *Slow Reading* (Duluth, Minn.: Litwin Books, 2009), p. 31.
[53]Ibid.
[54]Wen Stephenson, "The Internet Ate My Brain," *Boston Sunday Globe*, June 6, 2010, p. K6.

cognitive skills of awareness, attentiveness and concentration that can be transferred profitably to our other daily activities.

SCIENTIFIC STUDIES OF MEDITATION
HEALTH, MEDICINE AND NEUROSCIENCE

Any argument—such as the present one—for the recovery of a *Christian* practice of meditation today needs to take into account the rapidly increasing body of scientific studies of meditation and advances in neuroscience that have taken place since the 1950s. Insofar as these studies shed light on how the brain processes words and images, how the brain stores memories and how prayer and meditation affect the brain, they may yield important insights that can be integrated with a biblical and theological understanding of Christian meditation.

During the 1950s researchers conducted brain studies of practitioners of yoga in India and of Zen meditators in Japan; during the 1970s hundreds of studies were conducted in the United States on practitioners of Transcendental Meditation.[55] Since the 1990s these studies have been broadened to include further research on Zen Buddhist, Tibetan Buddhist, Theravada Buddhist (Vipassana), Hindu, Chinese, (Tai Chi; Qi Qong) and Christian forms of meditation, and academic researchers at various leading universities have focused on the interface between neuroscience and spiritual practices.[56] Notable in this regard were the "Mind and Life" meetings at MIT in 2003, and a November 2005 meeting cosponsored by the Georgetown School of Medicine and the Johns Hopkins School of Medicine, bringing together for dialogue the Dalai Lama, other Buddhist scholars, and neuroscientists.[57]

The growth of this research has been fueled by a convergence of

---

[55]Anoine Lutz, John D. Dunne and Richard J. Davidson, "Meditation and the Neuroscience of Consciousness: An Introduction," in *The Cambridge Handbook of Consciousness*, ed. Philip David Zelazo, Morris Moscovitch and Evan Thompson (Cambridge: Cambridge University Press, 2007), p. 530. This chapter is an excellent review of the current state of neuroscientific studies of meditation.

[56]The most extensive documentation of neuroscientific studies of Zen meditation is found in James H. Austin, *Zen and the Brain: Toward an Understanding of Meditation and Consciousness* (Cambridge, Mass.: MIT Press, 1998). Austin is professor emeritus of neurology at the University of Colorado Health Center and a Zen practitioner.

[57]Ibid.

several cultural factors: new advances in scientific instrumentation, such as functional magnetic resonance imaging (fMRI); the influx of Eastern religions into the United States since the 1960s; the growing appetite for various forms of "spirituality" and meditative practices; and the burgeoning interest in the connections between spirituality and health.

The technique of electroencephalography (EEG), which measures electrical potentials on the human scalp, was first used in 1929 and has been continuously used, especially since the 1950s, in studies of meditation and brain activity.[58] Since the 1990s functional magnetic resonance imaging (fMRI) techniques have been the instruments of choice for many neuroscientists studying meditation, for this technology enables the researcher to track blood flow in the brain in real time and to determine which parts of the brain are being activated as the subject thinks, feels and reacts to external stimuli or engages in meditative practices.[59]

Awareness by the general public of the interface between neuroscience and meditation is largely the result of a growing body of research on the connections between spiritual practices, including meditation, and physical and emotional health. A pioneer in this area has been Dr. Herbert Benson, a faculty member of the Harvard Medical School, and author of the bestselling book *The Relaxation Response* (1975). Using his studies of practitioners of Transcendental Meditation, Benson adapted this Eastern practice to secular contexts and argued that ten to twenty minutes of daily meditative practice, involving a quiet environment, the repetition of a meaningful word or phrase, a passive attitude and a comfortable position could produce significant health benefits such as stress reduction and decreased risks of high blood pressure, heart attack and stroke.[60]

Since Benson's pioneering efforts in the 1970s the therapeutic use of meditation in medical settings has become mainstream in the United States, with many researchers supporting the claim that meditation can be beneficial to health.[61] In the Oxford *Handbook of Religion and*

---

[58]Ibid., p. 531.
[59]Ibid., p. 540.
[60]Herbert Benson, *The Relaxation Response* (New York: Avon Books, 1975); a new and updated edition was published in 2000.
[61]A slight caveat, however, would seem to be in order in evaluating the claims to follow; note, for

Health, for example, Harold Koenig, Michael McCullough and David Larson give extensive documentation of studies on the use of meditation in the treatment of coronary heart disease, hypertension and substance abuse.[62]

Dr. Andrew Newberg of the Center for Spirituality and the Mind at the University of Pennsylvania, based on his neuroscientific research over the last thirty years, concluded that meditation and intensive prayer can "permanently strengthen neural functioning in specific parts of the brain that are involved with lowering anxiety and depression, enhancing social awareness and empathy, and improving cognitive and intellectual functioning."[63] Meditation can activate neural connections that protect the brain from some of the negative effects of aging and stress, and also give greater control over the emotions.[64]

The mainstream nature of Newberg's neuroscientific research on meditation and spiritual practices is reflected by the existence of a growing number of such mind-body research centers around the country: the Duke University Center for Spirituality, Theology, and Health; the Center for Spirituality and Health at the University of Florida; the Institute for Religion and Health at the Texas Medical Center; the Center for Mindfulness at the University of Massachusetts; the University of Virginia Mindfulness Center; and the Center for Spirituality and Healing at the University of Minnesota, to name only a few.[65]

---

example, a meta-analysis of 813 studies on meditation and health, focusing especially on hypertension, cardiovascular disease and substance abuse, published by the United States National Center for Complementary and Alternative Medicine, that concluded that "Scientific research on meditation practices does not appear to have a common theoretical perspective and is characterized by poor methodological quality. Firm conclusions on the effects of meditation practices in healthcare cannot be drawn based on the available evidence" and called for further research ("Meditation Practices for Health: State of the Research," Rockville, Md., Agency for Healthcare Research and Quality, June 2007, p. v, www.mentalhealthwatch.org/reports/meditation.shtml. This is not to discount the considerable evidence for positive health effects of meditation, but indicates that caution is in order.

[62]Harold G. Koenig, Michael E. McCullough and David B. Larson, *Handbook of Religion and Health* (Oxford: Oxford University Press, 2001), pp. 176-79; 247-48; 260-62.

[63]Andrew Newberg, *How God Changes Your Brain: Breakthrough Findings From a Leading Neuroscientist* (New York: Ballantine, 2009), p. 149.

[64]Ibid., pp. 149-50.

[65]Ibid., p. 255.

Evangelical Christians should not let suspicions concerning "Eastern" meditation blind them to this growing body of scientific research that links meditative practices to significant health and emotional benefits, but rather should ask, how can this research be integrated into my own Christian beliefs and spiritual practices?[66]

NEW DEVELOPMENTS IN BIBLICAL AND SYSTEMATIC THEOLOGY

In addition to the broader cultural factors already discussed, there are important internal developments within the broader community of theological scholarship that make a fresh investigation of the foundations of Christian meditation timely at the present moment: the growing recognition of the fragmentation of theological education and the renewed interest within theological circles in the themes of inaugurated eschatology, trinitarian theology and union with Christ. These latter themes have yet to be fully integrated into the historic practice of Christian meditation; and an attempt to provide such an integration is one of the chief purposes of this book.[67]

In his seminal critique of theological education in America, *Theo-*

---

[66]A recent and noteworthy example of an attempt to do this is the book by Curt Thompson, *Anatomy of the Soul: Surprising Connections Between Neuroscience and Spiritual Practices That Can Transform Your Life and Relationships* (Carrollton, Tex.: SaltRiver/Tyndale House, 2010). Thompson is a practicing psychiatrist and evangelical Christian, and connects neuroscientific research to relational and emotional health.

[67]Earlier studies of biblical meditation by evangelical authors such as Edmund P. Clowney, *Christian Meditation* (Nutley, N.J.: Craig Press, 1979); Campbell McAlpine, *The Practice of Biblical Meditation* (London: MarshallPickering, 1981); Walter C. Kaiser Jr., "What Is Biblical Meditation?" in *Renewing Your Mind in a Secular World*, ed. John D. Woodbridge (Chicago: Moody Press, 1985); Peter Toon, *The Art of Meditating on Scripture* (Grand Rapids: Zondervan, 1993) provide helpful biblical and practical insights but do not engage with the recent scholarship in the areas of inaugurated eschatology, trinitarian theology and union with Christ that are being addressed here.

The following works, representing a variety of theological perspectives, likewise contain worthwhile practical and historical insights, but do not address the issues of systematic and biblical theology investigated in the present essay: Morton T. Kelsey, *The Other Side of Silence: A Guide to Christian Meditation* (New York: Paulist Press, 1976) [Episcopal; Jungian psychology]; Ken Kaisch, *Finding God: A Handbook of Christian Meditation* (New York: Paulist Press, 1994 [Episcopal; "progressive": "Simply open your *awareness* so that you can experience the Divine Presence directly, without the blinders of belief," p. 57]; William E. Hulme, *Let the Spirit In: Practicing Christian Devotional Meditation* (Nashville: Abingdon, 1979) [mainline Protestant; pastoral psychology].

logia: The Fragmentation and Unity of Theological Education, Edward Farley pointed to the transformation of theology into an Aristotelian, university-based "science" in the thirteenth century as a watershed in the way that ministers were to be trained for service in the church.[68] Heretofore, theology had been conceived of as a "habitus" or disposition of the soul directed toward communion with God, a "holy wisdom" that was not primarily an academic or scientific object of study. This changed with Aquinas and the schoolmen and the introduction of Aristotelian logic and dialectic into the medieval universities. The very fact that this transition "occurred in the universities and not in institutions presided over by bishops or abbots," noted Farley, "created a new distance between theology and the church."[69]

In modern settings, where church ministry is often conceived of in largely institutional and administrative terms (programs, committees and ministerial functions), theology ceases to be a "holy wisdom" and disposition of the soul, and becomes systematic theology, a set of courses in a seminary curriculum: specialized, technical knowledge for the minister that may or may not have deep connections with the minister's own spiritual formation.[70] For over seven hundred years, it would seem, theology and "spirituality" have been going their separate ways, with academic theologians paying scant attention to the life of the soul, and those concerned with the life of the soul and personal devotion finding little sustenance from academic theology. This present essay is a modest attempt to bring these two critical elements in the life of the church closer together, so that robust biblical theology nurtures spiritual practice, and spiritual practices are informed by a sound and robust theology.

In the third chapter of this book I propose a fresh integration of three important themes in modern theological scholarship into the his-

---

[68]Edward Farley, *Theologia: The Fragmentation and Unity of Theological Education* (Philadelphia: Fortress Press, 1983), p. 38. At the time of writing, Farley was professor of theology at Vanderbilt University.

[69]Ibid.

[70]Ibid., pp. 43-44: "Its older usage ["theology," *theologia*] as a disposition of the soul toward God has been transformed . . . into know-hows for the tasks of ministry. . . . It is not too strong to say that the theological school will make little progress in understanding its present nature and situation if it overlooks the disappearance of the very thing which is supposed to be its essence, agenda, and ethos" (ibid.).

toric practice of biblical meditation: trinitarian theology, inaugurated eschatology and union with Christ. With respect to trinitarian theology, it should be noted that the modern renaissance of interest in the doctrine of the Trinity, generated largely but not exclusively by the formative work of Karl Rahner in Catholic circles and Karl Barth in Protestant circles in the last century, has yet to be fully integrated into the spiritual practices of the clergy and laity.[71] Evangelical Protestants, who are prone, and understandably so, to have a Jesus-centered spirituality, can be profitably reminded that Christian faith is a *trinitarian* faith, and that salvation in the fullest sense is fellowship with God the Father through Jesus Christ the Son in the communion with the Holy Spirit.[72] Meditating on Scripture, with faith and by the Spirit, brings us into the living presence of God Father, Son and Holy Spirit.

Since the early twentieth century, and especially subsequent to the publication of Albert Schweitzer's seminal work of 1906, *Von Reimarus zu Wrede* (Eng. trans., *The Quest of the Historical Jesus*), New Testament scholars have increasingly recognized the central and pervasive role of *eschatology* and the *kingdom of God* in the preaching of Jesus, and in New Testament theology generally. It is now widely recognized that Jesus announced the advent of the reign and power of God, and that through his life, death and resurrection, ascension, and the coming of the Spirit at Pentecost, the "powers of the coming age" (Heb 6:5) were already present in the church, though only to be fully realized at the end of

---

[71]For a review of recent scholarship in trinitarian theology, see Fred Sanders, "The Trinity," 35-53, in *The Oxford Handbook of Systematic Theology*, ed. John Webster, Kathryn Tanner and Iain Torrance (Oxford: Oxford University Press, 2007). Significant recent contributions in this area include Catherine LaCugna, *God for Us: The Trinity and Christian Life* (San Francisco: HarperSanFrancisco, 1973); Jürgen Moltmann, *The Trinity and the Kingdom* (Minneapolis: Fortress Press, 1993); Leonardo Boff, *Trinity and Society* (Maryknoll, N.Y.: Orbis, 1988); Thomas F. Torrance, *The Christian Doctrine of God: One Being Three Persons* (Edinburgh: T & T Clark, 1996); John D. Zizioulas, *Being as Communion* (Crestwood, N.Y.: St. Vladimir's Seminary Press, 1993); and John D. Zizioulas, *Communion and Otherness* (London: T & T Clark, 2007).

[72]My colleague Donald Fairbairn has called fresh attention to the trinitarian character of Christian life and salvation in his recent book *Life in the Trinity: An Introduction to Theology with the Help of the Church Fathers* (Downers Grove, Ill.: IVP Academic, 2009). James Torrance called attention to the fact that the doctrine of God in liberal Protestantism was essentially unitarian: "With this moralistic, individualistic understanding of God, the doctrine of the Trinity loses its meaning, in fact disappears—and with it the doctrines of atonement and unconditional free grace, held out to us in Christ" (James B. Torrance, *Worship, Community & the Triune God of Grace* [Downers Grove, Ill.: InterVarsity Press, 1996], p. 26).

history.[73] This New Testament inaugurated eschatology, and the reality of the "already, not yet" presence of the kingdom and Spirit, has important theological implications for spiritual practices such as meditating on Scripture that have yet to be adequately integrated with devotional practice.[74]

The "already" presence of the kingdom and Holy Spirit means that communion with the living God, in faith and through the Scriptures, can have a new depth of richness and immediacy that was not yet the case in the old covenant. The implications of this inaugurated eschatology call for more serious reflection and application, especially in the wake of the historic outpourings of the Holy Spirit on churches around the world since the Azusa Street revival of 1906, which birthed the most dynamic and rapidly growing segment of today's world Christian movement. Inaugurated eschatology and the presence of the Spirit are no longer merely scholarly concerns, but spiritual realities that continue to reshape the life and worship of the global church.

Since the publication in 1930 of Albert Schweitzer's *Die Mystik des Apostels Paulus* (Eng. trans., *The Mysticism of Paul the Apostle*), New Testament scholars have increasingly recognized (and debated) the "mystical" dimensions of Paul's theology, but have struggled to make sense of such Pauline notions as being "in Christ," laboring, I believe, under the weight of the naturalistic and scientific categories of the Enlightenment and the scientific revolution.[75] The realities of inaugurated eschatology

---

[73]For a helpful overview and survey of recent scholarship on New Testament eschatology generally, and in particular, so-called "inaugurated eschatology" of the "already-not yet," see Greg K. Beale, "The Eschatological Conception of New Testament Theology," in *Eschatology in Bible and Theology*, ed. Kent E. Brower and Mark W. Elliott (Downers Grove, Ill.: InterVarsity Press, 1997), pp. 11-52, esp. p. 13 n. 2 for additional bibliography of scholarly literature on the topic.

[74]Subsequent to the pioneering work of scholars such as Oscar Cullmann, *Christ and Time* (London: SCM Press, 1951), evangelical scholars such as George Eldon Ladd expounded the themes of eschatology and the kingdom of God in works such as *The Gospel of the Kingdom* (Grand Rapids: Eerdmans, 1959) and *The Presence of the Future* (Grand Rapids: Eerdmans, 1974). More recently, N. T. Wright, *Surprised By Hope: Rethinking Heaven, the Resurrection, and the Mission of the Church* (New York: HarperCollins, 2008) argues that an eschatology of resurrection and new creation is at the heart of the New Testament message.

[75]For a helpful survey of the history of modern New Testament scholarship on the Pauline notions of "in Christ" and union with Christ, see William B. Barcley, *"Christ in You": A Study in Paul's Theology and Ethics* (Lanham, Md.: University Press of America, 1999), pp. 5-19. See also James S. Stewart, *A Man in Christ: The Vital Element of St. Paul's Religion* (London: Hodder & Stoughton, 1947).

and union with Christ are not unrelated, of course; they are both consequences of the resurrection of Christ and the outpouring of the Spirit on
the church.

In the second section of this book I propose a fresh understanding
of the metaphysics of the Pauline notion of union with Christ, drawing
on insights from the inaugurated eschatology of the New Testament,
the presence of the Spirit and some new analogies from cyberspace and
Internet technology that provide new ways of understanding how
persons can be present to one another. This enhanced understanding of
union with Christ can provide, I believe, an enhanced experience of
communion with the risen Christ in the practice of biblical meditation.
Additionally, I will argue that the twin realities of inaugurated eschatology and union with Christ give grounds for retrieving the ancient
fourfold sense of Scripture—especially the christological and heavenly
senses, inasmuch as the presence of the kingdom opens a way of access
to Christ in the heavenlies (Eph 2:6; Heb 10:19-22) and to heaven itself
(Eph 2:6; Col 3:1-2; Heb 12:22-24) that was not yet possible under the
old covenant.

> Train yourself to be godly. . . . [It holds] promise for the both present life
> and the life to come. (1 Tim 4:7-8)

Having surveyed the current cultural landscape within which the
Bible is read (or not being read) today, we are in a position to suggest
that an enhanced, meditative reading of Scripture can offer the following very real benefits: (1) a pathway to a more personally transformative engagement with the Word of God, which does not replace
sermons or Bible study but enhances both; (2) a biblically and theological robust meditative practice that has a clear *Christian* identity in
the face of Buddhist and other Eastern spiritual practices; (3) a means
of enhancing knowledge of Scripture in the face of growing biblical
illiteracy in the culture; (4) a valuable way of maintaining and strength-
ening the cognitive skills of attentiveness and concentration in the
midst of an Internet culture of information overload and distraction; (5)
a way of integrating the scientifically proven health benefits of meditation into our own spiritual disciplines; (6) a means of applying im-

portant new theological insights (for example, concerning eschatology and union with Christ) in spiritually powerful ways.

It is my hope that this essay will be, in part, an answer to the concern voiced by the evangelical scholar Glen Scorgie, a professor of theology at Bethel Seminary San Diego, some years ago concerning the lack of integration in many evangelical churches and seminaries between the academic study of the Bible and vibrant spirituality. "There continues to be," he noted, "a perceived dissonance in approaches to Scripture between formal evangelical hermeneutics and the active listening encouraged by the meditative tradition."[76] As long as this dissonance continues to exist, the best that churches and seminaries can do is to offer "biblical studies courses on the one side and spiritual formation courses on the other" and hope that the people are able to integrate these disconnected pieces of the puzzle themselves; all too often the result is an "unfortunate kind of Christian schizophrenia."[77]

This book, with its proposal for a whole-brain method of biblical meditation, is an attempt to offer a solution to this problem. In chapters three through five I will present theological foundations for an enhanced Christian meditative practice, focusing on the themes of inaugurated eschatology, the Trinity and union with Christ. In the sixth and final chapters I will present some specific, practical methods for applying these principles in daily Bible meditation.

---

[76]Glen Scorgie, "Hermeneutics and the Meditative Use of Scripture: The Case for a Baptized Imagination," www.bethel.edu/~gscorgie/articles/hermeneutics_med_use_of_script.htm.
[77]Ibid.

3

The Arrival of
the Age to Come

New Intimacy with God

~~~
~~~

THE CENTRAL THESIS OF THIS BOOK is that a believing,
prayerful and receptive reading of Scripture is an act of communion
with the triune God, who is really present to the reader through and
with the biblical text. This chapter will set out a constructive theological proposal in support of this thesis, with special emphasis on the
following three theological themes: inaugurated eschatology, union
with Christ and communion with the Holy Trinity. The working assumption of the chapter is that while these theological truths may be
implicit in the traditional practices of biblical meditation, they have not
yet been fully integrated into those practices in an intentional and fully
conscious way. Meditative practices that originated in the desert spiri-
tualities of the early church, and that were continued and further developed in the Benedictine tradition of the West and the Orthodox
monasticism of the East, achieved canonical forms long prior to the
modern Protestant theological scholarship on such topics as inaugurated eschatology, and hence could not have been incorporated into
these practices. This chapter attempts to bring together in an integrated
way the best of ancient (Catholic) practices and the best theological
insights of modern Protestant biblical scholarship.

The constructive theological proposal in this chapter will first explore the themes of inaugurated eschatology, union with Christ and communion with the triune God, with a view to their implications for a meditative reading of Scripture. In chapter four I will argue that these three theological themes form the basis for a comprehensive biblical *worldview* or fundamental ontology that provides a framework or cognitive paradigm within which Scripture should be read. Chapter six will explore the *hermeneutical* implications of the foregoing discussion, arguing in particular for a modern retrieval of the ancient fourfold sense of Scripture and a fresh appreciation of the ancient church's understandings of *metaphor*, *symbol* and *imagination* in the meditative reading of the Bible.

THE FATHER'S REAL, INTIMATE PRESENCE WITH HIS PEOPLE

The writer of the epistle to the Hebrews assumes without debate that his readers are among those who have already experienced the "powers of the age to come" (Heb 6:5 NRSV). As previously noted, this "inaugurated eschatology" of the "already, not yet" has been increasingly recognized by biblical scholars as a fundamental, indeed perhaps *the* fundamental perspective of New Testament theology.[1] In the life, death, resurrection and ascension of Jesus Christ, and sending of the Holy Spirit, God the Father has begun to fulfill the end-time events foretold by the Old Testament prophets: the ingathering of the exiles of Israel, the calling of the Gentiles, the proclamation of forgiveness of sins to his people and the renewed presence of the Holy Spirit in power and glory among the people of God.

Modern New Testament scholarship has repeatedly drawn attention to the pivotal nature of these eschatological events for the New Testament writers. The resurrection of Jesus Christ is not merely the resuscitation of a dead body—as extraordinary as that indeed is—but rather the beginning of a radically new order of existence for humanity and the world. In the words of Oscar Cullmann, the mighty Christ event of the resurrection has given "a new center to time" itself, the decisive victory over sin and death *already* having been won, yet not fully consummated until the end.[2]

---

[1]See literature cited in notes 72-73 of chap. 2.
[2]Oscar Cullmann, *Christ and Time* (London: SCM Press, 1951), p. 86.

As C. Marvin Pate has noted, for the apostle Paul the resurrection of Jesus Christ inaugurated the dawning of the age to come.[3] For Paul, the early Christians are those upon whom the "ends of the ages have come" (1 Cor 10:11 NRSV). The promised kingdom of the Messiah has now been inaugurated with the exaltation of Jesus to the right hand of the Father and is now being shared with believers (1 Cor 15:23-28); the promised bestowal of the Holy Spirit on *all* God's people (Joel 2:28-32) has been actualized by the sending of the Spirit by God the Father and God the Son on the day of Pentecost ("Exalted to the right hand of the God, he [Jesus] has received from the Father the promised Holy Spirit and has poured out what you now see and hear" [Acts 2:33]).

Richard B. Gaffin has convincingly argued that the resurrection of Christ is *the* pivotal factor in the entirety of the apostle Paul's teachings on salvation: "Not only is the resurrection . . . the climax of the redemptive history of Christ; it is also that from which the individual believer's experience of redemption derives its . . . inexhaustible fullness. . . [T]he resurrection . . . constitutes him [Christ] as life-giving Spirit to those joined to him."[4]

The renewed interest in the inaugurated eschatology of the New Testament has also led to recognition of the pervasive presence of the Holy Spirit in the New Testament and early Christianity—a natural consequence of the fact that a central aspect of the arrival of the age to come is the attendant arrival of the Holy Spirit among God's people in a way that transcends the old covenant. The new age of Messiah is at the same time the "age of the Spirit" in the life of the church.

In the history of theology, pneumatology (the doctrine of the Holy Spirit) has not received the same sustained attention as have doctrines such as the person of Christ or justification.[5] This has begun to change, however, since the early twentieth century, reflecting the impact of the

---

[3]C. Marvin Pate, *The End of the Ages Has Come: The Theology of Paul* (Grand Rapids: Zondervan, 1995), p. 79.

[4]Richard B. Gaffin Jr., *The Centrality of the Resurrection: A Study in Paul's Soteriology* (Grand Rapids: Baker, 1978), p. 135.

[5]For a comprehensive survey of the doctrine of the Holy Spirit in church history, based on a detailed knowledge of the primary sources, see the masterful three-volume work of Yves Congar, *I Believe in the Holy Spirit* (New York: Seabury, 1983).

Azusa Street revival and the remarkable global growth of Pentecostalism.[6] Nineteenth-century conservative Protestants such as R. A. Torrey emphasized a "baptism" of the Holy Spirit, focusing on empowerment for witnessing and service, and modern Pentecostalism has emphasized glossolalia (tongues) as the outward sign of the "baptism," but for the purpose of this book, the central focus will be on the presence of the Spirit as the reality of a new *intimacy and joy in communion with God.* Two aspects in particular of this new access to God will be noted later: the people of God as a *living temple* of the Holy Spirit, and the Holy Spirit as the Spirit of *adoption* and presence of the love of God in the believer's heart (Rom 5:5).[7]

BROUGHT NEAR BY THE SPIRIT
TEMPLE OF GOD, "*ABBA,* FATHER"

As noted earlier, a crucial consequence of the inbreaking of the age to come is the giving of a new, deeper, richer experience of the Holy Spirit to the people of God: all God's people are "charismatics" now, in the sense of being people of the Holy Spirit. "If anyone does not have the Spirit of Christ, he does not belong to Christ. . . . by him we cry, '*Abba,* Father'" (Rom 8:9, 15). "Because you are sons, God sent the Spirit of his Son into our hearts, the Spirit who calls out, '*Abba,* Father'" (Gal 4:6). The new experience of the Spirit, following on the glorification of Jesus ("Up to that time, the Spirit had not been given, since Jesus had not yet been glorified" [Jn 7:39]) in his death and resurrection, has profound implications for how the Bible is read, and for how we view ourselves as readers of the Bible.

Reading and meditating on Scripture in the alreadiness of the Spirit now present in the church means that a new depth of intimacy with God is possible under the new covenant. This new closeness in our re-

---

[6]On the resurgence of interest in the doctrine of the Holy Spirit, see Veli-Matti Kärkkäinen, "Introduction to Pneumatology as a Theological Discipline: A Pneumatological Renaissance," in *Pneumatology: The Holy Spirit in Ecumenical, International, and Contextual Perspective* (Grand Rapids: Baker Academic, 2002), pp. 11-13; see also Frank D. Macchia, *Baptized in the Spirit: A Global Pentecostal Theology* (Grand Rapids: Zondervan, 2006).

[7]The "baptism" of the Holy Spirit understood as a profoundly transformative experience of the love of God was central, of course, in John Wesley's teaching. See, for example, Charles W. Carter, *The Person and Ministry of the Holy Spirit: A Wesleyan View* (Grand Rapids: Baker, 1974); and Harald Lindstrom, *Wesley and Sanctification* (Grand Rapids: Zondervan, 1980).

lationship to God can be seen in two New Testament teachings—the Christian and the church as new temple of God, and the reality of "*Abba,* Father" and our adoption as beloved children of God.

Living into the "ordinary supernatural." Before proceeding to reflect on these two concepts, however, a word of explanation and caution concerning use of the term *charismatic* is in order. For many people in churches today, the term *charismatic* understandably conjures up associations such as "speaking in tongues" or "prophecy" or other *extraordinary* manifestations of the Spirit. I am not a cessationist on the gifts of the Holy Spirit, but I would urge you, the reader, to consider the concept of the *ordinary supernatural* when thinking about the ministry of the Holy Spirit. Texts such as John 20:22 (Jesus "breathed on them [the disciples] and said, 'Receive the Holy Spirit'") and Acts 1:2 ("giving instructions *through the Holy Spirit* to the apostles he had chosen" [emphasis added]) show that in the ministry of Jesus, after the resurrection, his Spirit-empowered ministry (Acts 1:2, teaching; Jn 20:19-23, commissioning the apostles for a ministry of forgiveness and reconciliation) was *not* in these cases accompanied by extraordinary manifestations, that is, healings, flames of fire, bodily shakings and the like.

The best image of the "ordinary supernatural" presence of the Holy Spirit is that of the gentle, quiet *dove* that descended on Jesus at his baptism in the Jordan River, empowering him for ministry and communicating to him as beloved Son the love of the Father—not an explosive stick of *dynamite* that can "explode" in churches! We do receive energy and power with the Spirit, but this power is constructive, not destructive. God wants churches to *grow* up—not to blow up!

In Acts 1:2 and John 20:22-23 we see that the invisible, quiet, but very real, presence of the Spirit (the ordinary supernatural) empowered the disciples to understand, remember and to obey Jesus' teachings and instructions, and gave these teachings a transformative impact beyond the natural energy of a human teacher. God still acts in the extraordinary supernatural in the church, but the key to a healthy church and Christian life is to operate consistently in the *ordinary supernatural*, in conscious dependence on the Holy Spirit, as we preach, meditate on Scripture and do the work of ministry generally.

Notice then the remarkable fact in the New Testament that because the Spirit has been poured out, and because the age to come has dawned, believers no longer just *go to* a temple where God is present, but themselves have *become* a temple where God feels personally at home and lives in intimate contact with his people.[8] The apostle Paul makes the remarkable claim that the local church, and the individual believer, are both the new end-time temple of God, in which God personally dwells by his Spirit ("your body is a temple of the Holy Spirit" [1 Cor 6:19]; "You yourselves [the Corinthian assembly] are God's temple and . . . God's Spirit lives in you" [1 Cor 3:16]).

Quite significantly, as C. Marvin Pate has pointed out, the apostle Paul chooses the specific term *naos*, which means the actual shrine or sanctuary of the deity, and not the more generic term *hieron*, used of the temple and its precincts, to refer to the Christian's body and the local church as temple.[9] In the old covenant, only Moses went into the immediate presence of God on Mount Sinai or the wilderness tabernacle, and only the high priest was to enter into the holy of holies in the Jerusalem temple once a year on the Day of Atonement.

Most remarkably, in the new covenant, in the age of the Spirit, *every believer* can be as close to God—indeed, closer (!)—than Moses was under the old covenant. As the writer of Hebrews states it, having earlier noted the presence of the powers of the coming age (Heb 6:5), "we have confidence to enter the Most Holy Place by the blood of Jesus . . . let us draw near to God with a sincere heart *in full assurance of faith*" (Heb 10:19, 22, emphasis added). The pivotal realities of the *atoning blood of Jesus* and the *presence of the Spirit* make possible a new access to God and greater intimacy with God in worship, in personal devotion and in the meditative reading of Scripture.

The other crucial new covenant truth that I want to highlight here is

---

[8]For a comprehensive study of the theme of temple in biblical theology, see G. K. Beale, *The Temple and the Church's Mission: A Biblical Theology of the Dwelling Place of God* (Downers Grove, Ill.: InterVarsity Press, 2004). For ancient Near Eastern backgrounds on the Old Testament concept of the temple as the "home" and dwelling place of the deity, see Jeffrey J. Niehaus, *Ancient Near Eastern Themes in Biblical Theology* (Grand Rapids: Kregel, 2008), esp. pp. 99-110, "Image: Divine Presence in the Temple."

[9]Pate, *End of the Ages Has Come*, p. 152.

that of *sonship* and *adoption*. "Because *you* are sons, God has sent the Spirit of his Son into our heart, the Spirit who calls out, '*Abba*, Father'" (Gal 4:6). "You received the Spirit of sonship, and by him we cry '*Abba*, Father.' The Spirit himself testifies with our spirit that we are God's children" (Rom 8:15-16). With the dawning of the age to come and the arrival of the Holy Spirit, the Spirit is now duplicating in the hearts of believers the prayer language of Jesus, in which God the Father Almighty can be known and addressed in the intimate language of "dear Father."

According to the New Testament scholar Joachim Jeremias, there are no examples in Palestinian Judaism where an individual person addresses God as "my Father."[10] It was revolutionary when Jesus dared to take this step, notes Jeremias, "to speak with God as a child speaks with his father, simply, intimately, securely. There is no doubt then that the *Abba* which Jesus uses to address God reveals the very basis of his communion with God."[11]

In the history of theology, because of the Reformation controversies between Rome and the Reformers, the doctrine of justification received a great deal of attention, but the doctrines of *adoption* and sonship have received relatively little. J. I. Packer in recent years has tried to correct this imbalance a bit, going even so far as to claim that "Our understanding of Christianity cannot be better than our grasp of adoption" and that adoption is "the highest privilege that the gospel offers; higher than justification."[12] I agree with Packer's estimation that adoption is "higher" in the sense that it expresses a more personal and intimate relationship with God. The forensic language of the courtroom, of being pardoned by the judge, is perfected and completed with the familial language of the home: the forgiving judge in the courtroom adopts us as his own and welcomes us joyfully to a happy home (cf. Lk 15:20-25, the Father's welcome to the prodigal son).

---

[10]Joachim Jeremias, *The Central Message of the New Testament* (New York: Charles Scribner's, 1965), p. 16. "Nowhere in the literature of the prayers of ancient Judaism . . . is this invocation of God as *Abba* to be found, neither in the liturgical nor in the informal prayers" (ibid., p. 19).

[11]Ibid., p. 21.

[12]J. I. Packer, *Knowing God* (Downers Grove, Ill.: InterVarsity Press, 1973), pp. 182, 186. Older theological studies of adoption that are still worth consulting include R. S. Candlish, *The Fatherhood of God* (Edinburgh: Adam and Charles Black, 1865); R. A. Webb, *The Reformed Doctrine of Adoption* (Grand Rapids: Eerdmans, 1947); and John Mackintosh Shaw, *The Christian Gospel of the Fatherhood of God* (London: Hodder & Stoughton, 1925).

Both the images of temple and adoption, then, point to a new intimacy and closeness to God inaugurated by the advent of the Spirit. We can approach God—and meditate on the Scriptures—not as those who are distant from God, but as those who are closer to God than Moses was in the tabernacle. We are now not only servants of God, but as our dear *Abba*-Father's beloved sons and daughters we are *really close* to God, spiritually and emotionally, and can share the embrace of the Son in the very bosom of the Father (cf. Jn 1:18; Lk 15:20, the returning prodigal son embraced by the father; Gal 4:6, "Because *you are* sons . . . '*Abba*, Father'").

UNION WITH CHRIST
REAL PRESENCE, ALL THE TIME

Because we are united to Christ in our conversion by the Holy Spirit, God is *really present* to us in the prayerful, meditative reading of Scripture: this is the central claim concerning union with Christ in relation to biblical meditation that will be explored in this section. "For we were all baptized by one Spirit into one body. . . . He who unites himself with the Lord is one with him in Spirit" (1 Cor 12:13; 1 Cor 6:17). The Holy Spirit is like an umbilical cord that unites us to Christ, and through which he imparts his life to us, like a vine to the branches (Jn 15:5).

The purpose here is to retrieve the concept of union with Christ (mystical union) from an exclusively future, *not-yet* view of Christian experience to the *already* of the present, from the margins of evangelical spirituality back toward the center, from the realm of the only metaphorical toward the metaphysically and truly real, and from the aspirations of a spiritual elite toward a normative spiritual foundation for every Christian.

Union with Christ, to be understood within the broader framework of inaugurated eschatology (resurrection, exaltation of Christ, outpouring of the Spirit at Pentecost), is a pervasive theme in the New Testament, being especially prominent in the Pauline and Johannine writings. We are "in Christ" as a result of his resurrection, his outpouring of the Holy Spirit (Acts 2:33), and our being united to him in his body by the Holy Spirit (1 Cor 6:17). The following New Testament texts indicate that the believer's union with Christ was (1) planned by the Father from eternity, (2) taught and promised by Christ the Son before his death and resurrection, and (3) effectuated by the Holy Spirit after Pentecost at the believer's conversion:

Union with Christ
Planned by the Father from eternity

> He chose us in him before the creation of the world. (Eph 1:4)
> [preexistence of the mystical union and body of Christ in eternity past]

Union with Christ
Taught and promised by Christ before the cross and resurrection

> On that day you will realize that I am in my Father, and you are in me, and I am in you. (Jn 14:20)

> My Father will love him, and we will come to him and make our home with him. (Jn 14:23)

> I am the vine; you are the branches. (Jn 15:5)

> I have given them the glory that you gave me, that they may be one as we are one: I in them and you in me. [*perichorēsis*] (Jn 17:22-23)

> I have made you known to them, and will continue to make you known in order that the love you have for me may be in them and *that I myself may be in them*. [purpose of divine revelation: participation in the trinitarian love of the Father for the Son] (Jn 17:26, emphasis added)

Union with Christ
Effected by the Holy Spirit after Pentecost at conversion

> All of us who were baptized into Christ Jesus were baptized into his death. (Rom 6:3)

> Our old self was crucified with him. (Rom 6:6)

> We were buried with him through baptism. (Rom 6:4)

> We died with Christ. (Rom 6:8)

He who unites himself with the Lord is one with him in spirit. (1 Cor 6:17)

For we were all baptized by one Spirit into one body. (1 Cor 12:13)

If anyone is in Christ, he is a new creation; the old has gone. (2 Cor 5:17)

I have been crucified with Christ and I no longer live, but Christ lives in me. (Gal 2:20)

Having believed, you were marked in him with a seal, the promised Holy Spirit. (Eph 1:13)

God, who is rich in mercy, made us alive with Christ. (Eph 2:4-5)

God raised us up with Christ and seated us with him in the heavenly realms. (Eph 2:6)

In him you too are being built together to become a dwelling in which God lives by his Spirit. (Eph 2:22)

In him . . . we may approach God with freedom and confidence. (Eph 3:12)

We will in all things grow up into him who is the Head, that is, Christ. (Eph 4:15)

If you have any encouragement from being united with Christ. (Phil 2:1)

In commenting on the significance of these texts, Thomas Oden has observed that the living, spiritual union with Christ of which they speak cannot be adequately viewed merely as the cooperation of workers in a common task or a union of mind between student and teacher, but must be conceived in more organic categories, such as the members of a living body, living branches in a vine or the loving marital union of husband and wife. "Mechanical analogies fall short of describing organisms," notes Oden. "Without loss of individuality, the spirit of the person is enlivened by Christ, so that 'he who unites himself to the Lord is one with him in spirit' (1 Cor 6:17)."[13] Union with Christ is not just a metaphor; because the Holy Spirit is *real*, the bond between Christ and the believer by the Spirit is real—a real "umbilical cord" by which Christ pours his life and his love into us.

---

[13]Thomas C. Oden, *Classic Christianity: A Systematic Theology* (New York: HarperOne, 1992), p. 654.

The theme of the believer's union with Christ is a pervasive theme in the church fathers,[14] and as Louis Dupre has pointed out, "the assumption of a Christian experience of God's presence in all devout believers persisted in the West well into the thirteenth century and in the East much longer."[15] The mystical spiritual sensibilities of Eastern Christianity, it seems, were more hospitable to the biblical reality of the believer's mystical union with Christ than were the more forensic and judicial theological categories of the Western churches.

The growing marginalization of union with Christ as a normal experience for all believers in the medieval and modern periods could be attributed to a number of different historical and theological developments, including the rise of scholastic theology in the universities, with the emphasis on logic and dialectics; the rise of the doctrine of transubstantiation, with its localization and externalization of the *real presence* of Christ in the communion wafer; the growing clericalization of the church, with the priest understood as the essential mediator of the grace of Christ; and the lack of the Scriptures in the vernacular, and consequent lack of teaching of the biblical doctrine of union with Christ.

While the mainstream Reformers were suspicious of the "enthusiastic" and potentially disruptive spiritual experiences of some Anabaptists, and equally suspicious of any forms of Catholic mysticism that might displace the centrality of sovereign grace with human work, they nevertheless affirmed the historic biblical and patristic teachings concerning union with Christ. Luther strongly affirmed the reality of the believer's union with Christ, stating that "Faith . . . unites the soul with Christ as a bride is united with her bridegroom. . . . [T]he believing soul can boast of and glory in whatever Christ has as if it were its own."[16] In recent years Lu-

---

[14]For representative patristic citations on union with Christ, see "Union with Christ and Sanctification," in ibid., pp. 651-55, see also the citations listed in W. A. Jurgens, *The Faith of the Early Fathers* (Collegeville, Minn.: Liturgical Press, 1979), 3:377, on "Habitual Grace: The Supernatural Order," and the "indwelling Holy Spirit"; becoming a "sharer in the divine nature"; and becoming "adoptive sons of God."

[15]Louis Dupre, "The Christian Experience of Mystical Union," *Journal of Religion* 69 (1989): 2. Dupre points out that the term *mystic* was not used prior to the sixteenth century to refer to a particular individual or class in the church who had unusual mystical experiences.

[16]Martin Luther, "A Treatise on Christian Liberty," cited in Hugh T. Kerr, *A Compend of Luther's Theology* (Philadelphia: Westminster Press, 1966), p. 58.

theran scholars in Finland have argued for the recognition of a more central place for union with Christ in Luther's theology.[17]

Calvin spoke very forthrightly about the reality of union with Christ: "To sum up, the Holy Spirit is the bond by which Christ effectually unites us to himself . . . to share with us what he has received from the Father, he had to become ours and dwell within us . . . all that he possesses is nothing to us until we grow into one body with him."[18] Union with Christ is real and not just a metaphor because the *Holy Spirit is real*—and not just a metaphor. "Christ is not outside us but dwells within us," says Calvin. "Not only does he cleave to us by an indivisible bond of fellowship, but with a wonderful communion day by day, he grows more and more into one body with us, until he becomes completely one with us."[19]

The Westminster Confession of Faith (1646), a benchmark of the English-speaking Reformed tradition, treats the topics of effectual calling (10), justification (11), adoption (12) and sanctification (13), but, unlike Calvin, makes no explicit mention of union with Christ. This omission may reflect the predominantly forensic categories of the tradition of covenant theology that it represents. Union with Christ is, however, explicitly mentioned in Q.66 of the Westminster Larger Catechism: "The union which the elect have with Christ is the work of God's grace, whereby they are spiritually and mystically, *yet really and inseparably* [emphasis added], joined to Christ as their head and husband, which is done in their effectual calling."[20]

Union with Christ is a prominent theme in the theology of Puritan writers such as William Perkins, John Bunyan, Richard Baxter, Thomas

---

[17]For an overview and discussion of the so-called "New Finnish" interpretation of Luther, see Carl E. Braaten and Robert W. Jenson, eds., *Union with Christ: The New Finnish Interpretation of Luther* (Grand Rapids: Eerdmans, 1998). According to Tuomo Mannermaa of the University of Helsinki, many modern German Luther scholars were unduly influenced by the nineteenth-century philosopher Hermann Lotze, whose insistence that all metaphysics must be grounded in the natural sciences undercut the ontological categories on which union with Christ in Luther needs to be understood.

[18]John Calvin, *Institutes of the Christian Religion* 3.1.1, "The Holy Spirit as the Bond That Unites Us to Christ."

[19]Ibid., 3.2.24. For further discussion of union with Christ in Calvin, see Wilhelm Niesel, *The Theology of Calvin* (Philadelphia: Westminster Press, 1956), pp. 120-26; and Ronald S. Wallace, *Calvin's Doctrine of the Christian Life* (Edinburgh: Oliver & Boyd, 1959).

[20]*The Confession of Faith and Catechisms* (Willow Grove, Penn.: Committee on Christian Education of the Orthodox Presbyterian Church, 2005), p. 203.

Goodwin, John Flavel and John Owen.[21] This is not surprising, given the Puritan concern to combine biblical orthodoxy with a lively experiential piety. Upon his conversion John Bunyan, in his *Grace Abounding*, affirmed that the Lord had led him into "the mystery of union with this Son of God, that I was joined to him, that I was flesh of his flesh, and bone of his bone."[22] Tudor Jones has stated that for the Puritans union with Christ "is not to be understood as the achievement of a few heroic souls but a divine gift received by all true Christians."[23] In the Puritan view, union with Christ stood at the beginning of the Christian life, not just at its end; the basis for communion with God and with other Christians was none other than union with Christ.[24]

Reformed theologians in the post-Reformation period continued to recognize the fundamental place of union with Christ in the plan of salvation.[25] For Robert L. Dabney, a leading nineteenth-century theologian of the southern Presbyterian Church, the bond of the mystical union of Christ and his people was the Holy Spirit, who "literally unites Christ and his people," who dwells in them and maintains in them "by supernatural power . . . the same spiritual life, which exists in the Head."[26] Dabney's reference to "supernatural power" in reference to union with Christ should not be missed. "In a word," continued Dabney, "there is truly a sap, a cement which unites the two, that is a thing, and not merely an influence—a divine, living, and Almighty Person, viz.: Holy Ghost."[27] The mystical union is clearly for Dabney not merely a metaphor or figure of speech or only a legal relation, but rather a real

---

[21]See the fine study by R. Tudor Jones, "Union with Christ: The Existential Nerve of Puritan Piety," *Tyndale Bulletin* 41, no. 2 (1990): 186-208, for the references that follow.

[22]John Bunyan, cited in ibid., p. 187.

[23]Jones, "Union with Christ," p. 192.

[24]Ibid., p. 187.

[25]For a helpful survey and analysis of union with Christ in the Reformed tradition from the time of the Reformation to the present, see Michael S. Horton, "Mystical Union in Reformed Soteriology," in *Covenant and Salvation: Union with Christ* (Louisville: Westminster John Knox Press, 2007), pp. 129-52. Horton attempts to bring together the participationist ("in Christ") and forensic dimensions of union with Christ. According to Horton, in "classic Reformed treatments" Christ is the sole basis for both justification and union, but "the act of justification is logically prior to union" (ibid., p. 147).

[26]Robert L. Dabney, *Lectures in Systematic Theology* (1878; reprint, Grand Rapids: Zondervan, 1972), p. 616.

[27]Ibid.

and substantial relation by virtue of person and presence of the Holy Spirit—the third person of the Trinity.

B. B. Warfield, the notable theologian of "Old Princeton," most often remembered for his stalwart defense of the inspiration and authority of the Bible, spoke and wrote warmly about union with Christ. In one of his Sunday afternoon addresses to seminary students on the subject of "Communion with Christ," Warfield spoke about the "Christian's union with Christ and its abiding effects." Because we are united with Christ in his death and resurrection, we "live in him and through him"; the Christian is a "new creation, with a new life in him; and should live in the power of this new and deathless life."[28] For Warfield this union with Christ was the basis for a true evangelical and Christian "mysticism," reflecting the realities of the indwelling Holy Spirit and the Christ within, leading to newness of life within the soul and leading the newly regenerated soul "along the pathway of holy living."[29]

John Murray, for many years professor of systematic theology at Westminster Theological Seminary in Philadelphia, highlighted the place of union with Christ in his widely read treatment of the plan of salvation, *Redemption: Accomplished and Applied*. For Murray union with Christ is not some isolated, inert, spiritual "factoid," but a momentous reality that "embraces the wide span of salvation from its ultimate source in the eternal election of God [Eph 1:4] to its final fruition in the glorification of the elect [Rom 8:30]. . . . [I]t underlies every aspect of redemption both in its accomplishment and its application."[30] Murray was a careful and judicious Scotsman and scholar, and not given to overstatement; let the reader note and reflect on the sweeping nature of this claim!

For Murray the believer's union with Christ is "mysticism on the highest plane. . . . It is the mysticism of communion with the one true and living

---

[28]B. B. Warfield, *Faith and Life* (1916; reprint, Carlisle, Penn.: Banner of Truth, 1974), p. 422.

[29]B. B. Warfield, *Studies in Theology* (1932; reprint, Grand Rapids: Baker, 1981), p. 654. For Warfield an evangelical and biblical form of mysticism is one in which religious experience is tested by and subject to the authority of Scripture; unbiblical forms of mysticism substitute "religious experience for the objective revelation of God recorded in the written word" (ibid., pp. 654-55).

[30]John Murray, *Redemption: Accomplished and Applied* (Grand Rapids: Eerdmans, 1955), p. 165.

God." It is a mysticism of communion with the triune God, Father, Son and Holy Spirit, "that union with Christ draws along with it."[31] Murray goes on to speak of the *affective* and emotional dimensions of the believer's union with Christ in terms that echo the lyrical heights of the medieval mystics at their best: union with Christ "stirs the deepest springs of emotion in the raptures of holy love and joy."[32] *Raptures of holy love and joy*: is this a Calvinism without heart and emotion? A joyless orthodoxy? Surely not!

It is apparent from this brief survey that the Reformed and Puritan theological tradition recognizes a central and vital place for union with Christ in the plan of salvation and the Christian life. The upshot of the foregoing discussion, in the context of this essay on biblical meditation, is that the reader of the Bible comes to the text not as a stranger to Christ—who is the central subject of all Scripture—but as one who is actually connected to Christ by the Holy Spirit, as one who is really in the *real presence* of the risen Lord in the prayerful reading of Scripture. Meditating on Scripture can and should be a real-time experience of communion with the living Christ.

It is a peculiar and lamentable fact, then, that in much of today's popular evangelical piety and preaching this great New Testament truth of union with Christ appears to have little traction and prominence in the understanding and experience of the gospel. For many in the evangelical tradition, a tradition that speaks easily of a "personal relationship with Christ," a vivid sense that *already* we are in living communion with Christ—not merely waiting to be united to Christ in heaven when we die—seems to be missing. Could this be a reflection of the pragmatic, activistic temperament of much American evangelicalism, which tends to be suspicious of forms of spirituality that are perceived as being "mystical" or "Catholic"?

One should not be too hard on popular evangelicalism in this matter, however, because scholars and theologians—not just the laity—have struggled to make sense of the mystical language of the apostle Paul, and such concepts as being in Christ, of being crucified and raised with Christ, and being "seated with Christ in the heavenly

---

[31]Ibid., p. 172.
[32]Ibid., p. 173.

realms" (Eph 2:6). As previously noted, since the pioneering work of Albert Schweitzer these eschatological and participationist notions in Pauline theology have been recognized by scholars as being decisive for Paul, but there has been no consensus as to how to interpret them and how to relate them to the categories of modern thought.[33]

In one of the finest modern studies of union with Christ, Alfred Wikenhauser, a Roman Catholic New Testament scholar at the University of Freiburg, Germany, has demonstrated that for the apostle Paul, union with Christ is "something real, an objective state" that is "true of all [Christians] without exception."[34] The apostle considers it a "self-evident fact," notes Wikenhauser, "that as soon as a man becomes a Christian he enters upon this vital union with Christ," and "Christ and his followers are bound in a mysterious union of intimate fellowship in life and being."[35] This union is not a fusion of two persons, but a union of Christ and the believer where each preserves his or her personality.[36]

Wikenhauser stresses the *objective* character of union with Christ for Paul: this fellowship with Christ is not "a momentary experience which occurs at times of high spiritual exaltation; it is a reality, an objective fact that does not depend on the perception of the operations of Christ. It is true, of course," he notes, "that these operations can be perceived, but *they are real whether we notice them or not.*"[37]

Union with Christ, then, is not merely an ethical category, it is *ontological:* the apostle Paul, concludes Wikenhauser, uses phrases such as "in Christ" to express his deep conviction that "the Christian lives on a plane where his life is profoundly influenced by a divine power,

---

[33]For a review of modern scholarly discussions of the Pauline "Christ in you/me" language, see William B. Barcley, *"Christ in You": A Study in Paul's Theology and Ethics* (Lanham, Md.: University Press of America, 1999), pp. 5-19.

[34]Alfred Wikenhauser, *Pauline Mysticism: Christ in the Mystical Teaching of St. Paul* (London: Nelson, 1960), p. 93. Other studies of this topic that could be mentioned include Lewis B. Smedes, *All Things Made New: A Theology of Man's Union with Christ* (Grand Rapids: Eerdmans, 1970); J. Todd Billings, *Calvin, Participation, and the Gift: The Activity of Believers in Union with Christ* (Oxford: Oxford University Press, 2007); and Robert C. Tannehill, *Dying and Rising with Christ: A Study in Pauline Theology* (Berlin: Topelmann, 1967). In my view, the work of Wikenhauser provides the most incisive discussion and recognition of the clearly *ontological* dimensions of the apostle's thought.

[35]Wikenhauser, *Pauline Mysticism*, pp. 93, 92.

[36]Ibid., p. 184.

[37]Ibid., p. 108 (emphasis added).

and where to some degree the very quality of his life has been changed (see esp. 2 Cor 5:17)."[38]

The question remains, however, of just how to understand, in the light of a modern worldview informed by the sciences, such an onto-logical basis for the mystical union. E. P. Sanders could be named as a prominent biblical scholar who recognizes the mystical or participa-tionist dimensions of Pauline theology but struggles to make sense of it. For Sanders, the participationist categories of the "in Christ" language bring us closer to the heart of Paul's thought than do the juridical or forensic categories and "reveal the depth of it."[39] Sanders disagrees with Bultmann's existentializing interpretation of Paul, and his comments are worth extensive quotation:

> It seems to me best to understand Paul as saying what he meant and meaning what he said: Christians really are one body and Spirit with Christ, the form of the present really is passing away, Christians really are being changed from one stage of glory to another, the end really will come and those who are in Christ will really be transformed.[40]

But then Sanders goes on to ask:

> But what does this mean? How are we to understand it? We seem to lack a concept of "reality"—a real participation in Christ, real possession of the Spirit—which lies between naïve cosmological speculation and belief in magical transference on the one hand [for example, Gnosticism or Hellenistic mystery religions] and a revised self-understanding [for ex-ample, Bultmann] on the other. *I confess that I do not have a new category of perception to propose here.*[41]

Sanders recognizes that neither the ancient categories of Gnosticism, Hellenistic mysteries or magical thought, nor a modern Bultmannian interpretation reflecting Kant's exclusion of divine action and presence from the external world, are adequate for understanding Paul's concept

---

[38]Ibid., pp. 32, 63, 64.

[39]E. P. Sanders, *Paul and Palestinian Judaism*, p. 520, cited in John Ashton, *The Religion of Paul the Apostle* (New Haven, Conn.: Yale University Press, 2000), p. 150; see chap. 4, "Paul the Mystic," and "Excursus III: Schweitzer's *Mysticism*," pp. 113-51.

[40]Ibid., p. 150.

[41]Ibid. (emphasis added).

of being "in Christ," but he offers no alternative ontological categories of his own. Understandably, like many scholars in the modern and postmodern periods, assumptions about reality dominated by modern science and technology—for example, the "real" is that which is visible, material and knowable by the scientific method—hinder Sanders from understanding a Pauline reality that supervenes upon but at the same time transcends that which is visible and material in nature.

I will offer such an "ontological alternative" later, based on the premise that Paul's encounter with the risen Christ on the Damascus road produced a radical paradigm shift *that fundamentally altered Paul's understanding of reality*—inaugurated eschatology, in effect, being the genesis of a new Pauline ontology and epistemology. This new ontology will be proposed by introducing new notions of the self, new concepts of how persons can be present to one another, and a fundamental premise that *invisible spirit* must be recognized as having metaphysical and causative primacy over the visible and the material dimensions of creation. Analogies from modern science, technology and cyberspace will be invoked to illustrate and argue for the plausibility of such an inaugurated ontology of the new creation, a new reality *already* operating in the world since the resurrection of Jesus and arrival of the Spirit.

Before sketching out such an inaugurated ontology, however, we need to notice developments in recent trinitarian theology that are related to the foregoing discussions of eschatology and union with Christ, and that have important implications for biblical meditation understood as an act of communion with God who is really present.

TRINITARIAN GOD, CHRISTIAN MEDITATION

Having considered in the previous sections inaugurated eschatology, with its prominent theme of the arrival of the *Spirit* in fullness, and having considered union with Christ the *Son*, the second person of the Trinity, it is appropriate at this point to consider, at least briefly, the doctrine of the Trinity—God who is *Father*, Son and Holy Spirit—in relation to biblical meditation.

We have already noted in the second chapter the modern renais-

sance of interest in the doctrine of the Trinity across wide sectors of
the church—Protestant, Roman Catholic and Eastern Orthodox.[42]
This new interest in the Trinity reflects not only the scholarly efforts
of Karl Barth, Karl Rahner and other theologians, but also the new
prominence of the Holy Spirit in the global church and the growth of
the worldwide Pentecostal and charismatic movements.[43] Scholars
have been exploring this new awareness of the centrality of the Trinity
for the Christian faith and its practical implications for worship and
personal spirituality.

Many Christians think of the doctrine of the Trinity as an esoteric
puzzle they should believe, but which has little practical significance
for Christian living; this is not really the case, however.[44] At the very
least the biblical teachings concerning the triune nature of God provide
essential *background information* for all aspects of the life of the church
and Christian faith. If you visit an art museum with an exhibit that
features Rembrandt's *The Night Watch* and other Dutch masters, the
more background information you bring with you about seventeenth-
century Dutch culture, history and religion, the more likely it is that
you will enjoy and appreciate Rembrandt and *The Night Watch* at a
deeper and richer level. So it is with the spiritual life: a deeper understanding of God can help us have a richer relationship with God and
communion with God when we meditate on Scripture.

---

[42]Chap. 2, n. 71. Some of the literature referenced there includes Catherine LaCugna, *God For Us: The Trinity and Christian Life* (San Francisco: HarperSanFrancisco, 1973); Jürgen Molt-mann, *The Trinity and the Kingdom* (Minneapolis: Fortress Press, 1993); Leonardo Boff, *Trinity and Society* (Maryknoll, N.Y.: Orbis, 1988); Thomas F. Torrance, *The Christian Doctrine of God, One Being Three Persons* (Edinburgh: T & T Clark, 1996); John D. Zizioulas, *Being as Com-munion* (Crestwood, N.Y.: St. Vladimir's Seminary Press, 1993); and John D. Zizioulas, *Com-munion and Otherness* (London: T & T Clark, 2007).

[43]The growth of the church in the Global South and the prominent place of Pentecostalism in that growth has been documented by Philip Jenkins, *The Next Christendom: The Coming of Global Christianity* (Oxford: Oxford University Press, 2002).

[44]The historic, orthodox doctrine of the Trinity and the biblical witness can be summarized in three simple statements: (1) There is one God and only one God [Christians do not believe in three gods]; (2) this one God exists eternally as Father, Son and Holy Spirit; (3) these three persons, Father, Son and Holy Spirit, are fully equal in nature, power and glory, each fully possessing the divine nature. These three statements do not attempt to explain the mystery but rather to preserve and express the biblical data in an accurate and balanced way. For a clear and succinct discussion see Roger Nicole, "The Meaning of the Trinity," in *One God in Trinity*, ed. Peter Toon and James Spiceland (Westchester, Ill.: Cornerstone, 1980), pp. 1-10.

The reality of God as Father, Son and Holy Spirit can enhance our meditation in three important respects: our view of God, our view of ourselves and our view of salvation. First, our view of God: to state the obvious, the quality of our relationship with a person is very much affected by the accuracy of our understanding of who that person really is. Two people can fall madly in love, get married and then discover that they were "in love with love," and married with very flawed understandings both of themselves and of their partner. A good marriage needs to be based on true perceptions of the other person, not on fantasies.

In the case of God, we remember that God said, "I Am Who I Am" (Ex 3:14)—"not necessarily who you *think* I am or who you would like me to be; I am who *I am*—and you may as well adjust your thinking and expectations accordingly." The God of the Old Testament, the great *I Am* of Mount Sinai, Yahweh the God of Israel, is more fully revealed in the New Testament as Father, Son and Holy Spirit. The triune God is the real God with whom we can have fellowship and communion as we meditate on the Scriptures with faith. As we meditate on Scripture, pray or worship in the church, the very salvation experience that we enjoy is a loving and joyful relationship not only with Jesus but also with the Father ("Our fellowship is with the Father *and* with his Son, Jesus Christ" [1 Jn 1:3]), in the communion of the Holy Spirit. Salvation involves having a healthy, enjoyable and close relationship with all three persons of the Trinity: with the Father, with the Son and with the Holy Spirit—being drawn into the circle of these three divine persons who are sharing their love, joy, peace and glory with us (cf. Jn 17: joy [v. 13], love [v. 23], glory [vv. 22, 24], peace [Jn 16:33]). The trinitarian God— Father, Son and Holy Spirit—is *inherently* relational, and hence our experience of God is trinitarian and relational in nature.

Second, with respect to our view of our selves, the doctrine of the Trinity is a crucial reminder that we as persons, created in the image of God, who is inherently relational in nature, were also created to have our true being in relationship to others. Father, Son and Holy Spirit are *distinct* persons, but not *separate* or *independent* persons. Father, Son and Holy Spirit always operate in partnership and cooperation with one another. Our persistent temptation as humans is to act independently of other persons and independently of God.

James Torrance is on the mark when he argues that in today's church what is needed is "a better understanding of the person not just as an individual but as someone who finds his or her true being in communion with God and others, the counterpart of a trinitarian doctrine of God."[45] I agree with Torrance's view that "The human person is someone who finds his or her true being in relation, in love, in communion."[46] Meditating on Scripture with a conscious understanding of the triune character of God, and of ourselves as persons created and redeemed for relationship with God and others, can help us to resist the rampant individualism of our culture, and reinforce our efforts to live in more relational and cooperative ways.

Third, with respect to our understanding of salvation and the Christian life, the doctrine of the Trinity reminds us that salvation itself is trinitarian in nature.[47] Salvation is not only or merely forgiveness of sins and going to heaven when we die—though it is certainly not less than that. There is a danger that evangelical spirituality can, in practice, be a "unitarianism of the second Person," being focused on Jesus alone to the neglect of the Father and the Spirit.

Salvation in the fuller and more biblical sense is sharing in ever deepening measure in the life of the triune God: participating in and enjoying, by and in the Holy Spirit, Jesus' joyous experience of his Father's love. Our experience of salvation is one of being "invited into the circle" of the love, joy and peace that the Father, Son and Spirit have enjoyed among themselves from all eternity.

Our destiny, the purpose for which we were designed and redeemed (Eph 1:4) is to enjoy, beginning now, and continuing into eternity in ever deepening measure, the measureless depths of the fullness of God's love (Eph 3:17-19). Our destiny is to enter into, in a finite and

---

[45]James B. Torrance, *Worship, Community and the Triune God of Grace* (Downers Grove, Ill.: InterVarsity Press, 1996), p. 38. Torrance's brief study is an excellent exposition of a biblical and trinitarian understanding of worship.

[46]Ibid., p. 39.

[47]As noted earlier, this important truth has been admirably stated by Donald Fairbairn, *Life in the Trinity: An Introduction to Theology with the Help of the Church Fathers* (Downers Grove, Ill.: IVP Academic, 2009).

analogous way that does not erase the Creator-creature distinction, the joyful, living relationship that the Father and the Son enjoy in the communion of the Holy Spirit.[48] Meditating on Scripture in faith can be a gateway and point of access through which we enter into this experience and trinitarian fellowship even now, in this life, in anticipation of an even deeper experience in the life to come.

EXCURSUS
HOW PERSONAL AGENTS ARE LOCATED IN SPACE
Extended Selves and Union with Christ

The title of this excursus, "How Personal Agents Are Located in Space," may appear to be rather abstract, but I would like to argue that the clarification and modification of some of our commonsense notions of "place" and "object" can shed light on some important theological issues: how God can be present with us in personal meditation and in corporate worship, how the risen Christ is "really present" during the celebration of the Lord's Supper, and how the believer is really, not just metaphorically, united to Christ.[49] This discussion is also an attempt to provide some further clarification to some of the notions advanced in my book *Worship and the Reality of God*, especially chapters three ("Reality in Worship: The Real Presence of God on Sunday Morning") and four ("The Eucharist: Meeting the Risen Christ at the Table").[50]

This exercise in the clarification of the metaphysics of place/location and object/self will be focused on a discussion of the following

---

[48]Drawing on the Christology of Cyril of Alexandria, Donald Fairbairn highlights Cyril's important distinction between *idios,* the communion that the Son has with the Father by virtue of the shared divine nature, and *oikiotes,* the (finite and analogous) fellowship or participation that we enjoy with the Father and the Son by the Holy Spirit; we enjoy fellowship with the Father and the Son, but our human natures remain distinct from the divine nature (Donald Fairbairn, "Grace As Sharing Divine Communion," in *Grace and Christology in the Early Church* [Oxford: Oxford University Press, 2003], pp. 63-104).

[49]Some readers may wish to skip this excursus and continue with chapter four, and then return to this excursus later. This philosophical analysis is intended to introduce some new concepts such as the *extended self* that can help us understand union with Christ and the Pauline language of being "in Christ" that was discussed on pp. 41-51. The material in this excursus was previously published. Permission has been granted by the editor of *Philosophia Christi* to reprint "How Personal Agents Are Located in Space," 13:2 (Summer 2011): 437-44. For more information about the journal, please visit epsociety.org.

[50]John Jefferson Davis, *Worship and the Reality of God* (Downers Grove, Ill.: IVP Academic, 2010).

key terms and distinctions: *definitive, circumscriptive* and *repletive* modes of presence of an object or self; the distinction between an *empirical* (or molecular) *self* and an *extended self;* and the notions of *supervenience* and *reception spaces* (or "encoding media"), to be explained. The discussion will conclude with an attempt to show how these terms and distinctions can shed light on some of the controverted issues in the history of theology, in regard to corporate worship, the Lord's Supper or Eucharist, and union with Christ.

Terminology. First, consider the distinction between the *circumscriptive* and *repletive* modes of presence of an object.[51] If I place my pet cat George in a carrying cage to take him to the veterinarian, George is *definitively* located at a certain place in space and not at another, and he is also *circumscriptively* located in the cage, in the sense of being contained or circumscribed within the boundaries of the cage. On the other hand, if on the way to the veterinarian, my smartphone rings and I answer it, then the electromagnetic radiation that brings my wife's message to pick up a gallon of milk at the store, while *definitively* present in my cell phone, is at the same time *repletively* present throughout the broadcast range of the Verizon network; it is not circumscribed to its presence in my receiver. A material particle has a definite location in space; energy, in the form of radiation, is "spread out."

In this respect the mode of presence of spiritual agents such as the Holy Spirit is, in significant respects, more like that of the electromagnetic radiation carrying the cell phone message than it is like that of George in his cage. On the day of Pentecost the Holy Spirit was *definitively* (and visibly) present in a specific location (Mount Zion, Jerusalem), and yet at the same time, *repletively* present throughout the world as well as in heaven, within the life of the Trinity.[52] The point to notice here is that the way that visible, molecular objects (or personal agents) are present in space does not exhaust the metaphysical possibilities of how an object or agent that is not (only) molecular in nature can be

---

[51]On the use of these terms in medieval scholastic theology, see Thomas M. Osborne, "Faith, Philosophy, and the Nominalist Background to Luther's Defense of the Real Presence," *Journal of the History of Ideas* 63, no. 1 (2002): 63-82.

[52]The Holy Spirit has the property of omnipresence, while the smartphone signal does not: its mode of presence is repletive or "spread out," but the range of reception is limited.

present in space. Our ordinary, commonsense experience of visible, material objects tends to reinforce our (unconscious) assumption that "real presence" is *circumscriptive* visible, molecular presence, but this notion is too limited to cover all the relevant cases, as the example of the smartphone message shows. How this observation can help us to understand statements of Christ such as "Where two or three come together in my name, there am I with them" (Mt 18:20) and "Surely I am with you always, to the very end of the age" (Mt 28:20) will be discussed shortly.

The next distinction that I wish to introduce is that between an *empirical* (or "molecular") *self* and an *extended self*. This notion of an "extended self" is itself an extension of an idea proposed by Andy Clark and David Chalmers in a seminal article in the philosophy of mind, "The Extended Mind."[53] Clark and Chalmers argue that it is fallacious to regard the mind as an entity that is only contained (circumscriptively) within the brain and the human body; the mind can be extended into the external environment by means of tools or other physical objects that serve the purposes of the personal agent. For example, consider the case of Otto, a man suffering memory loss from Alzheimer's disease; he supplements his memory by writing down the directions to the Museum of Modern Art on 53rd Street in New York in a notebook that he carries with him wherever he goes.[54] Otto's notebook, serving his purposes and under his control, is in effect an extension of his mind; his brain and the notebook are a "coupled system" that constitute his extended mind.

This notion of the extended mind can itself be extended to the notion of an *extended self*, and in a theological context to Christ and to the believer. In the incarnation, the Logos "extends" himself into a human body, and the Logos is *definitively* but not *circumscriptively* present in the body of Jesus of Nazareth; the Logos and the divine nature have the property of omnipresence, and are *repletively* present both in heaven and earth. Upon conversion, the believer is baptized into the body of Christ (1 Cor 12:13), and from that moment on is metaphysically "coupled" or "bonded" to Christ by the Holy Spirit, as

---

[53] Andy Clark and David J. Chalmers, "The Extended Mind," *Analysis* 58 (1998):10-23, http://consc.net/papers/extended.html.
[54] Ibid., p. 6.

really and truly as a Verizon customer is networked or connected to others in the Verizon network by the cell phones, electromagnetic waves and software that make these connections possible. In a similar way, we extend ourselves into cyberspace with our Facebook accounts: our Facebook homepages extend our three-dimensional molecular selves into cyberspace, and represent ourselves to others photonically in a two-dimensional *reception space* (that is, the computer screens of our Facebook "friends"). Our extended self in cyberspace is not molecular or three-dimensional but digital, but it is nevertheless "real," only real in a different mode.[55]

This Facebook analogy, and even more so the cases of Christ and the believer united in the body of Christ by the Holy Spirit, suggest—indeed seem to require—the enlarged notion of a *hybrid self* or "complex self" to account for some of the New Testament language of union with Christ that we will discuss: "seated . . . with [Christ] in the heavenly realms" (Eph 2:6) and so forth. It is here proposed that the believing Christian is no longer only an empirical, visible, molecular self, but in fact, an extended and *complex* self, metaphysically linked in the body of Christ by the Holy Spirit to Christ, the head of the body. This bond between the believer and Christ constituted by the Holy Spirit is a real and permanent relation. In this metaphysics both the Spirit is real and the relationship itself is real: the Head-body-Spirit-believer connection is not just a metaphor but an ontological reality, inaugurated by the resurrection of Jesus Christ, his ascension to heaven, the outpouring of the Holy Spirit and the incorporation of the believer into the body of Christ by the Holy Spirit at conversion.[56] This notion will be further developed later.

---

[55] Another illustration of the same notion of *extended self* is provided by Skype software; when we use Skype, we are extending ourselves into cyberspace and representing ourselves in real time into the two-dimensional reception space of our friends' computer screens: our molecular selves are definitively and circumscriptively present within our bodies and a particular geographic location; our extended/Skyped selves can be repletively (and digitally) present in many locations simultaneously.

[56] This notion of the Christian's *extended* and *complex self* is not to be confused with pantheism: Christ and the believer remain eternally distinct; the believer has and will continue to have a molecular and empirical body; the point, however, is that the believer really is a *new creation* and no longer a separate, autonomous individual, but one whose identity has been newly reconstituted through the Spirit's work of conversion and united the believer to the living Christ. The "new" metaphysical notions being proposed here are in fact nothing more than an attempt

The third set of terms that I wish to introduce to this discussion are those of *supervenience* and *reception spaces*. The notion of *supervenience*, that literally suggests a "coming upon from above," is introduced to call attention to the fact that the contact, presence and influence of one object or agent on another object or agent is not limited to a "molecular" mode of contact. When in a game of billiards the cue ball strikes the eight ball and sends it into the side pocket, this contact, presence and influence of one ball on another is "molecular," physical and visible. However, when my cell phone rings and I answer the call, a molecular object (the cell phone) is a *reception space* that is in contact with a non-molecular, invisible yet very real entity: the electromagnetic radiation that is carrying the message. The message (information) supervenes upon the cell phone and the computer chip that it contains; the information of the message and the cell phone itself are metaphysically not the same type of entities, and yet they have very real contact and interaction. In an analogous fashion the Holy Spirit supervenes on the soul/spirit of the believer (cf. "The Spirit himself testifies with our spirit that we are God's children" [Rom 8:16]). The human spirit of the believer is a "reception space" for the Holy Spirit; the Holy Spirit as a real, permanent broadband connection between the believer and Christ can be thought of as creating a spiritual Skype connection that represents the believer to Christ in the heavenly places (cf. "God raised us up with Christ and seated us with him in the heavenly realms" [Eph 2:6]). I will attempt to further unpack these notions shortly.

Implications for worship and biblical meditation. With respect to the question of how Christ is present during the act of corporate worship (and, by extension, in biblical meditation) it would seem that the concept of the *extended self* can help us understand some of the biblical statements (for example, "When you are assembled in the *name* of our Lord Jesus . . . and the power of our Lord Jesus is present" [1 Cor 5:4] or, "Where two or three come together in my *name*, there I am with them" [Mt 18:20]). Here it is evident that the "name" of Jesus is not just

---

to flesh out the implications of the *inaugurated eschatology* that is at the heart of the New Testament message of already arriving kingdom of God that is making all things new ("If anyone is *in Christ*, he is a new creation; the old has gone, the new has come" [2 Cor 5:17]).

a semantic marker that refers to a person who is absent but is a "verbal icon" that conveys the presence of the one to whom it refers (cf. "You are to seek the place the LORD your God will choose . . . to put his Name there for his dwelling. . . . There, *in the presence of the Lord your God*, you and your families shall eat and shall rejoice" [Deut 12:5, 7, emphasis added]). The "Name" of Yahweh or the risen Jesus, then, is an extension of God's own self. Jesus' extended self includes his "name" invoked in the midst of the worshiping assembly. Likewise, the Shekinah glory cloud that led Israel during the wilderness wanderings can be regarded as a manifestation of Yahweh's extended self; God's "hand" and "Spirit" are also extensions of his self. The Spirit of God, in the form of the Shekinah glory in the wilderness (cf. Is 63:11-14; Ex 14:19-22) was locally or definitively present in the glory cloud, but not circumscribed by it; the Spirit continued to have the property of omnipresence. The name, the Spirit, the glory of God can be regarded, so to speak, as God's "Skype icons" by which he extends his self/extended self into the midst of his people.

In regards to 1 Corinthians 5:4, then, Christ is present in the Corinthian house church assembly because his name and the Spirit extend his self into their midst. It is justifiable, in fact, to regard the Holy Spirit as, in a sense, an extension of Jesus' self (note the close association of "Lord" and "Spirit" in 2 Corinthians 3:17, "the Lord is the Spirit, and where the Spirit of the Lord is, there is freedom"), especially in light of the *perichorēsis* or mutual indwelling of the three divine persons (the Father in the Son, the Son in the Father, the Spirit in both). Because Jesus is in the Father and the Father in Jesus, Jesus can say to Philip, "Anyone who has seen me has seen the Father" (Jn 14:9). Because the Spirit is in Jesus and because Jesus is in the Spirit, then where the Spirit is, there also is the risen Jesus. The three divine persons are "in" one another (*perichorēsis*), but remain eternally distinct from one another.[57]

Finally, some observations with regard to union with Christ, in relation to the notions of extended and hybrid selves. This relates in particular to how we can understand the presence of God to us in biblical

---

[57]The ancient heresy of modalism denied the eternal distinctions between the three divine persons.

meditation, in relation to our union with Christ. As noted earlier, from the time of Albert Schweitzer, if not earlier, New Testament scholars have noticed the prominence of the mystical aspects of Pauline theology and his "in Christ" language but have struggled to relate this Pauline language to modern sensibilities, reflecting perhaps the lingering influence of the naturalistic and scientific categories of the Enlightenment.

How can Paul, as a molecular self, and the risen Christ, still presumably a molecular (though glorified) self, be said to be "in" one another? The answer proposed here is to regard *both Christ and the believer as extended, complex selves*—linked, or ontologically bonded, to one another by the Holy Spirit. Paul's old self has died; his personhood is now constituted by Christ living in him (Gal 2:20). For every believer, the Spirit witnesses with our spirits that we are sons, or children, of the Father (Rom 8:16); the Holy Spirit extends my spirit into the heart of the Father, and the Spirit extends the heart of the Father into my heart, as the Father pours his love into my heart through the Holy Spirit given to me (Rom 5:5). Christ is "in" me not in a molecular sense but by his Spirit, truly extending himself into my spirit. The heavenly Christ Skypes his extended self into my heart by the Holy Spirit, his real-time broadband connection. In this case, however, the Skype analogy of course has its limitations, because in Christ my connection with Christ is *more real*, not less real, than a Skype connection; the *Holy Spirit* is surpassingly more real and weighty than any mere points of light on a computer screen.

Both Christ and the believer are, in effect, extended and complex selves, extended perichoretically into one another through the bond of the Holy Spirit. The extended Self of Christ, by means of the Spirit, *supervenes* upon my spirit, and my spirit, by means of the Spirit, supervenes upon his—and so Christ is "in" me, and I am in Christ.

And what of the Pauline statement that we have been raised with Christ and seated with him in the heavenly places (Eph 2:6)? This truth is not merely metaphorical but can be understood with the help of the concepts of the extended and complex self. My molecular self is here on earth, circumscribed by my physical body, but the molecules of my body do not constitute the totality of my new self in Christ; the

Spirit extends my spirit and connects it to heaven itself; I am permanently bonded or connected to Christ himself as a member of his body.

As Calvin argued in the *Institutes* (in his discussion of the presence of Christ in the occasion of the celebration of Lord's Supper), "the Spirit truly unites things separated in space" (4.17.10). The suggestions being made in this brief excursus are, in effect, some of Calvin's ideas with illustrations from cyberspace technology and the new proposed terminology of *extended* and *complex* selves.

The background of this entire discussion has been the premise that the inaugurated eschatology of the New Testament—the resurrection of Jesus, his ascension and the coming of the Spirit—fundamentally alters the way we need to conceptualize categories such as the self and how selves relate to space and to one another.[58] "If anyone is in Christ, he is a new creation" (2 Cor 5:17), which suggests, I believe, that traditional metaphysical categories of place and person need to be revisited. Christians have *already* begun to experience the "powers of the coming age" (Heb 6:5). These revised notions can help us to understand how Christ can be *really present* to us as we meditate in faith on the Scriptures, being united to Christ by the Holy Spirit.

---

[58]See the discussions in Thomas F. Torrance, *Space, Time and Incarnation* (London: Oxford University Press, 1969), and also his *Space, Time, and Resurrection* (Grand Rapids: Eerdmans, 1976).

4

INAUGURATED ONTOLOGY

A Biblical Worldview for Biblical Meditation

〰〰
〰〰

In THIS CHAPTER I WILL ARGUE (1) that inaugurated eschatology provides the essential foundations for a new ontology and biblical worldview in the light of which the Scriptures should be read, and
(2) that the seeds of this new inaugurated ontology and worldview
were sown in Paul's encounter with the risen Christ in his Damascus
road conversion experience. As to the second, I believe that Seyoon
Kim was essentially correct in arguing in his book *The Origins of Paul's
Gospel* that the origins of the apostle's distinctive message and understanding of the gospel were not to be found in parallels with Hellenistic mystery religions, Gnosticism, Hellenistic Judaism and so forth,
but rather in his encounter with the risen Christ on the Damascus
road. According to Kim,

> The characteristics of Paul's doctrine of justification *sola gratia* and *sola
> fide* are due to his insights into the . . . law, human existence and man's
> relationship to God which he developed out of his Damascus road ex-
> perience. . . . [I]t was by seeing the risen and exalted Christ as the Son
> and image of God . . . that Paul developed his soteriological conception
> of the believers' being adopted as sons of God, their being transformed
> into the glorious image of Christ and their being made the "new man"
> or καινη κτισις [new creation] through their incorporation into Christ,
> the Last Adam . . . the new humanity. . . . It is clear that Paul's gospel

and apostleship are grounded . . . in the Christophany on the Damascus road. The Damascus event is the basis both of his theology and his existence as an apostle.[1]

Other New Testament scholars have contested Kim's thesis in the part or the whole, but I believe that Kim is fundamentally correct in seeing the *resurrection of Jesus Christ* and Paul's personal encounter with the risen Christ on the Damascus road as the great "paradigm shifter" both for his theology and more generally for his view of reality as a whole.[2]

For Paul, it is not too much to say that the resurrection and arrival of the Spirit changes everything and that the resurrection of Jesus Christ makes it necessary to revise all previously existing concepts of reality. Paul's encounter with the risen Christ changed his views of God, the world, the self, history and salvation. Paul knew that being "in Christ" meant that a person was a "new creation" (2 Cor 5:17); the old ontology was gone; a new ontology had come.

Paul's understanding of God was transformed from the (monotheistic) God of Abraham, Isaac and Jacob into a trinitarian understanding of God as Father, Son and Holy Spirit.[3] The world itself—"cosmology"—

---

[1]Seyoon Kim, *The Origin of Paul's Gospel*, 2nd ed. (Tubingen: J. C. B. Mohr, 1984), p. 332.

[2]Kim has summarized and further developed his thesis and also responded to his critics in his subsequent book *Paul and the New Perspective: Second Thoughts on the Origins of Paul's Gospel* (Grand Rapids: Eerdmans, 2002), esp. chap. 5, "Christ the Image of God and the Last Adam," pp. 165-213, and chap. 6, "2 Corinthians 5:11-21 and the Origin of Paul's Concept of Reconciliation." The pivotal place of the resurrection of Jesus Christ, and its implications for an entirely new view of reality has recently been argued in the magisterial work of N. T. Wright, *The Resurrection of the Son of God* (Minneapolis: Fortress, 2003). "The early Christians insisted that what had happened to Jesus was precisely something new; was indeed, *the start of a whole new mode of existence, a new creation.* The fact that Jesus' resurrection was, and remains, without analogy is not an objection to the early Christian claim. It is part of the claim itself. . . . [The resurrection] blasts its way through the sealed tombs and locked doors of modernist epistemology. . . . Indeed, the holding apart of the mental and spiritual on the one hand from the social, cultural, and political on the other, one of the most important planks in the Enlightenment platform, is itself challenged by . . . Jesus' resurrection" (ibid., pp. 712-13, emphasis added).

[3]See Gordon D. Fee, "Christology and Pneumatology in Romans 8:9-11: Reflections on Paul as a Trinitarian," in *Jesus of Nazareth: Lord and Christ*, ed. Joel Green and Max Turner (Grand Rapids: Eerdmans, 1994), pp. 312-31. Fee argues that Paul had become a "functioning Trinitarian," having had his Jewish understanding of God transformed by his saving experience of God as Father, Son and Holy Spirit. See also the important work of Richard Bauckham, *God Crucified: Monotheism and Christology in the New Testament* (Grand Rapids: Eerdmans, 1998), arguing that New Testament Christology was "high" from the start, with Jesus "at the right hand of God" (Ps 110:1) being integrated into the very core identity of Yahweh as revealed in the Old Testament. Bauckham argues that from this point of view later patristic trinitarian

had been changed for Paul; the world in its present form was passing away (1 Cor 7:31), to be replaced by a new physics, a new order of creation. Because of the resurrection of Christ and the arrival of the Holy Spirit, he could no longer think of the self or the human being in the old way. The new person in Christ was a new way of being a human being ("his purpose was to create in himself one new man" [Eph 2:15]). The new Christian self is not a separate and independent self, but one whose very existence and identity is that of being baptized into the body of Christ (1 Cor 12:13) and connected to Christ ("he who unites himself to the Lord is one with him in spirit" [1 Cor 6:17]) and to other Christians by the Holy Spirit.

Paul's understanding of time and history was fundamentally altered by his encounter with the risen Lord. The age to come was not merely a future reality to be anticipated, but a presently arriving (already) reality to be experienced now in the Spirit, and by faith in the name of Jesus (cf. "when you are assembled in the name of Jesus, . . . *and the power of the Lord Jesus is present*" [1 Cor 5:4, emphasis added]).[4]

Paul's soteriology or view of salvation was fundamentally changed: the paradigm was no longer Moses and the law, but Jesus and the Spirit. Salvation was not fundamentally a matter of "works of the law" but rather a matter of faith in Jesus as God's Messiah vindicated by his resurrection (cf. "He was delivered over to death for our sins and was raised to life for our justification" [Rom 4:25]), fundamentally a matter of a faith like Abraham's, who could believe that God gives life to the dead and "calls things that are not as though they were" (Rom 4:17). In light of the resurrection Paul understood that the covenant with Abraham had been fulfilled in Jesus' death and resurrection, and that the gift of the Spirit and the experience of the supernatural powers of the age to come came not by observing the law but through hearing with faith (Gal 3:5).

---

doctrine was not in tension with Jewish monotheism, but a natural development of it.

[4]It is not too much of a stretch to suggest that in early Christianity, every Sunday morning worship service (e.g., 1 Cor 5:4) was a "power encounter" with the risen Lord, by virtue of the presence and power of the Spirit, and in a sense, analogous to Paul's Damascus road encounter. Cf. "Here I am! I stand at the door and knock" (Rev 3:20), the risen Christ comes in the Spirit and Word and during the occasion of the eucharistic meal to be present to the believers in the church of Laodicea.

In sum, then, Paul's encounter with the risen Christ on the road to Damascus produced an inaugurated eschatology, which for him was the basis of an inaugurated ontology or comprehensive new paradigm of reality. In chapters four and five I will sketch in a more systematic way the outlines and essential features of such an inaugurated ontology or worldview for the following seven topics: (1) theology (God), (2) cosmology (world), (3) anthropology (humanity, or the self), (4) epistemology (knowledge), (5) soteriology (salvation), (6) axiology/teleology (values, purpose), and (7) bibliology (Scripture). The claim that I wish to advance is that such a new ontological paradigm—a paradigm or worldview that I believe to be the worldview of Paul and Jesus—is the proper one within which the Scriptures need to be read, understood and meditated upon.

THE IMPORTANCE OF WORLDVIEW

By *worldview* I mean a comprehensive framework or set of assumptions about the nature of the world, reality as a whole and humanity's place and purpose in relation to the world. Worldviews provide a set of background beliefs and assumptions by means of which human beings interpret and make sense of their experience.[5]

For example, consider three individuals who see a sick and dying beggar on the streets of Calcutta: a nun of the Sisters of Charity mission, a Hindu and a Marxist. Each person sees the same beggar, but through the lens of a different worldview. The Hindu sees an individual suffering the results of the bad karma of previous lives. The Marxist sees a person who suffers because of the class structures of capitalism and private property, reinforced by delusory religious beliefs. The Sisters of Charity nun sees a person who suffers as a result of the complex interactions of original, personal and social sins, and who needs the mercy and love of God in Christ.

---

[5]For an accessible introduction to the concept of worldviews, see James W. Sire, *The Universe Next Door: A Basic Worldview Catalog* (Downers Grove, Ill.: InterVarsity Press, 1976). See also David Naugle, *Worldview: A History of the Concept* (Grand Rapids: Eerdmans, 2002); and Ninian Smart, *Worldviews: Cross-Cultural Explorations of Human Belief* (Upper Saddle River, N.J.: Prentice-Hall, 2000). Consciousness of the pluralism of worldviews, and of the need for Christians to self-consciously understand their own in the face of the "Other" has increased in the modern, post-Christendom period, when the Christian West has increasingly encountered non-Western cultures and religions.

Since we are not always acting with a conscious awareness of our basic worldview assumptions, our actions can be out of accord with our professed values and convictions. For example, we can say that we are not materialists who believe that matter is the ultimate reality, and yet still get caught up in the consumerism of our culture, which reinforces the false belief that material possessions and wealth are the keys to human happiness and well-being. Consequently, it is very worthwhile to try to bring our fundamental Christian worldview assumptions to full conscious awareness in order to act more intentionally and consistently in accordance with them.

While it may seem unnecessary and somewhat "academic" to discuss philosophical issues of worldview in a book on meditation, I ask the reader's patience in this matter, because I believe that in the long run attention to such matters will strengthen and enhance our spiritual experience in meditating on Scripture.

What follows can only be a very introductory and inadequate attempt to sketch out major themes, each of which merits book-length treatments. The purpose here is merely to suggest some implications that I hope will enrich our personal practice of meditation.

THEOLOGY
TRINITY AS ULTIMATE REALITY

In a preceding section ("Trinitarian God, Christian Meditation") we have already noted that the Christian doctrine of the Trinity can inform our understanding of God, the self and salvation, and so enhance our experience of biblical meditation; there is no need to repeat that material here. The Christian view, if we attempted to summarize it in one sentence, might be expressed as follows: "The one, true and living God, the almighty Maker of heaven and earth, exists eternally as Father, Son and Holy Spirit, as three distinct but not separate divine persons who equally share the divine nature or essence, existing eternally in holy, loving, joyous, harmonious and glorious personal relationships."[6]

---

[6]See also chap. 3, n. 44 for the historic, orthodox and biblical view of the Trinity, summarized in three simple statements. On the historical development of the doctrine of the Trinity, see J. N. D. Kelly, *Early Christian Doctrines*, 2nd ed. (New York: Harper & Row, 1960); and R. P. C.

When we meditate on the Scriptures in faith, we can actually experience the *real presence* of the triune God, who is present to us through the Word and by the Spirit. In meditation we can experience real-time communion with God, our loving heavenly Father, the Father who welcomes and joyfully embraces the returning prodigal son (Lk 15:20). We can experience communion with Jesus, the eternally beloved Son of our Father, who experiences joy in being loved by the Father (cf. "at that time Jesus, full of joy through the Holy Spirit, said, 'I praise you, Father'" [Lk 10:21]). We can experience communion with the Holy Spirit, who pours the love of the Father for the Son and for us into our hearts ("God has poured out his love into our hearts by the Holy Spirit, whom he has given us" [Rom 5:5]).[7]

When I say "can experience," I do not mean that every time we meditate on Scripture we will have a powerful emotional experience of God's love; at times, there may only be a dim but nevertheless real sense of God's presence, and at other times, no such feelings at all. God is not under our control, and God always remains free to manifest himself and his love in the ways and times of his own sovereign choosing.

But God is really there even when we may not feel that he is there. There have been times when I have felt suddenly and unexpectedly flooded by the love of God—during my morning meditation, even driving in the car, or walking around the track at the Bennett Center gymnasium at Gordon College, meditating on Scripture—but I believe, by faith, that God is really there even when I do not feel his presence, because he has promised to be with us and to make his home with us (Jn 14:21). Like a

---

Hanson, *The Search for the Christian Doctrine of God* (Edinburgh: T & T Clark, 1988). For a helpful discussion of the meaning of *person* in trinitarian usage, see Walter Kasper, *The God of Jesus Christ* (New York: Crossroad, 1984), pp. 285-90, and "The Trinitarian Mystery of God," pp. 233-316, for a clear and rigorous discussion of the patristic and medieval trinitarian discussions. As used here the divine persons are three eternally distinct centers of individuality within the one divine nature.

[7]Alan J. Torrance argues persuasively, and I think correctly, that the Christian church's trinitarian language of God, in Scripture, sacrament, and worship not merely points to the Trinity but can be the means by which the believing community actually *participates* in the joyous life of the Trinity (see his *Persons in Communion: Trinitarian Description and Human Participation* [Edinburgh: T & T Clark, 1996]). See also Donald Fairbairn, *Life in the Trinity*, for the view that Christian *salvation* is in fact an ever-deepening experience of and sharing in the Father's love for the Son and the Son's joy in the Father's love, in the fellowship of the Holy Spirit.

sleeping infant in her mother's arms, we can be receiving love even when we are not consciously aware of the presence of the one who loves us.

For the Christian, the triune God is *ultimate reality*, the "bottom line" in our view of the real, the ontologically or metaphysically ultimate category "that which none more 'real' can possibly be conceived," to paraphrase Anselm. The doctrine of the Trinity is a bedrock metaphysical distinctive that sets the Christian faith apart from other world religions and competing worldviews. Judaism, Christianity and Islam are Abrahamic faiths that share a common monotheistic heritage, but only Christianity affirms a one God fully revealed as Father, Son and Holy Spirit: three divine persons in eternal, loving, holy communion.

As over against atheism, materialism and scientific naturalism, Christian trinitarianism affirms that matter is real and essentially good—but denies that matter is the ultimate metaphysical reality. God, who has existed eternally, and who is invisible spirit (Jn 4:24), created matter; matter and material forces (for example, natural selection) did not create God or the idea of God. This is a crucial truth for the Christian to keep in mind, because "common sense" and the consumerism of late industrial capitalism and the advertising industry are continually trying to convince us that *material* objects and possessions are the keys to human satisfaction, and that life's fulfillment is to be found in *this* world, rather than in a new creation from above.

The doctrine of the Trinity also distinguishes the Christian worldview from Hinduism and Buddhism.[8] In these Eastern religions, the metaphysically ultimate category—Brahman, nirvana, sunyata (emptiness)—is considered to be spiritual or nonmaterial in nature, but this meta-

---

[8]It is sometime said that there is a Hindu "trinity" of Brahma (creator), Vishnu (preserver) and Shiva (destroyer), but this is not a true parallel to the Christian Trinity, because these three Hindu deities are not considered to be eternally distinct but manifestations of one another (cf. *modalism*, from a Christian and trinitarian point of view); nor are the "incarnations" or "avatars" of Vishnu (e.g., in the form of Krishna) truly historical in character. As K. M. Sen has pointed out, "Unlike Christianity which accepts only one unique Divine incarnation in Jesus Christ, Hindus accept many incarnations of God" (*Hinduism* [New York: Penguin Books, 1961], p. 73 n. 1). The devotees of Vishnu and Shiva are in fact two distinct "denominations" within the broader Hindu family of religions. Cf. Klaus K. Klostermaier, "Lord Vishnu and His Devotees," and "Shiva: The Grace and Terror of God," *A Survey of Hinduism*, 2nd ed. (Albany: State University of New York Press, 1994), pp. 239-77.

physical ultimate is *impersonal* and without real distinctions.[9] This is one of the deepest questions in all of human philosophy and religion: is ultimate reality *personal* or *impersonal* in nature? For the Christian, *persons in loving relationships* are metaphysically ultimate; for the Buddhist and many Hindus, the idea of human or divine "personality" must finally be transcended in union with an impersonal absolute.

In relation to the heritage of Greek philosophy, which formed an important part of the context in which the early church and Christian theology developed, the Christian doctrine of the Trinity asserts that *person* is the ultimate metaphysical category, not an abstract concept of changeless Being (Parmenides) or an atomistic concept of matter (Democritus). "Being" is *personal* being, being-in-relationship.[10] There is no abstract concept of "Being" as such that is metaphysically or epistemically prior to the reality and being of the Triune God, Father, Son and Holy Spirit—persons eternally in loving, joyous, holy and glorious relationship.

The Christian doctrine of the Trinity, then, is the foundation of a Christian understanding of ultimate reality and has consequences for all Christian thought and practice, including meditation. As we shall see, the doctrine of the Trinity, which implies the primacy of invisible spirit over visible matter, will have important implications for how we understand a Christian epistemology (theory of knowledge) and other aspects of a biblical worldview.

COSMOLOGY
How Heaven Disappeared and How to Get It Back

The word *cosmology* is often used in the context of discussions of astronomy and the modern scientific understanding of the size and nature of the physical universe (or universes). In a broader sense cosmology (Greek *kosmos*, "world") refers to the world picture generally held in a

---

[9]On the variety of Buddhist understandings of the concepts of nirvana and sunyata ("emptiness" or the "Void"), see Walpola Rahula, *What the Buddha Taught*, 2nd ed. (New York: Grove Press, 1974) [Theravada Buddhist perspective]; Paul Williams, *Mahayana Buddhism: The Doctrinal Foundations* (London: Routledge, 1989); and Keith Yandell and Harold Netland, *Buddhism: A Christian Exploration and Appraisal* (Downers Grove, Ill.: IVP Academic, 2009).

[10]This fundamentally important insight has been argued in the seminal work of John D. Zizioulas, *Being as Communion* (Crestwood, N.Y.: St. Vladimir's Seminary Press, 1993).

particular culture at a given time, such as, for example, the Ptolemaic/ Aristotelian picture of a solar system with the earth at its center, which was the generally accepted cosmology in Western civilization up until the modern period.

In this section I would like to focus our attention for a while on a serious "disconnect" between a biblical cosmology and our modern sensibilities, that is, the powerful reality of *heaven* in New Testament theology and the growing sense of the *unreality* of heaven in the Christian mind and imagination in the modern period. My belief is that a healthy Christian spirituality and practice of biblical meditation need a recovery of the biblical reality of heaven, and that such a recovery will in itself be a source of further renewal in Christian spirituality, worship and mission.

In this initial and brief attempt to point the way to the recovery of a more biblical sense of the reality of heaven—a more *biblical cosmology*— that can undergird and enrich the practice of biblical meditation, we will first survey the rich New Testament witness to heaven (that is, new creation) as a powerful reality that is *already* arriving and which is *already* accessible by the Spirit to the believer in the life and worship of the church. Second, we will consider briefly some of the conditions in the modern world that have accelerated the disappearance of heaven from the Christian imagination. Third, we will then consider some conceptual resources and analogies from modern scientific cosmologies that can actually help us reconceptualize and reimagine the biblical heaven and new creation.

To begin, consider two texts that give us a window into the mind and imagination of the apostle Paul and his heavenly cosmology:

> Since, then, you have been raised with Christ, set your hearts on things above, where Christ is seated at the right hand of God. Set your minds on things above, not on earthly things. For you died, and your life is now hidden with Christ in God. (Col 3:1-3)

> God, who is rich in mercy, made us alive with Christ. . . . And God raised us up with Christ and seated us with him in the heavenly realms in Christ Jesus. (Eph 2:4-6)

In Colossians 3:1-3 Paul tells us that, because we have been joined to Christ not only in his death (through our baptism [Col 2:12], buried with him) but also in his resurrection, the *primary focus* of our consciousness and attention should not be on the visible things of earth but on the unseen realities of the heavenly world, because that is where Christ the Lord of all reality is—exalted at the right hand of God. In Ephesians 2:6 Paul makes the remarkable claim (incomprehensible to the naturalistic, Enlightenment mind) that we are *already*, in some mysterious but very real sense, in heaven, that we have *experiential access* to the reality of the new creation.

Paul's new creation cosmology is a consequence of his inaugurated eschatology: the reality-transforming impact of the death and resurrection of the Messiah, the coming of the Spirit in fullness, and the arrival of the powers of the age to come. As we shall see, to understand Paul's claims we need a concept of an *extended* and *complex self* (see the excursus of chap. 3 and also the following section on anthropology) to help us understand how in the apostle's mind the Christian, with respect to the visible, molecular self, is still very much on earth below, but with respect to the truer and fuller, extended self, by virtue of being bonded and linked to the risen Lord by the Holy Spirit, is also at the same time already truly located and extended into the heavenly world.

These texts are hardly the only New Testament witnesses to the reality of the unseen heavenly world. Consider the following texts that give us further insight into the minds of Jesus, John, Paul and the writer to the Hebrews:

In my Father's house are many rooms. . . . I am going there to prepare a place for you. (Jn 14:2)

The Jerusalem that is above is . . . our mother. (Gal 4:26)

Our citizenship is in heaven. (Phil 3:20)

They [Old Testament priests] serve at a sanctuary that is a copy and shadow of what is in heaven. (Heb 8:5)

Christ did not enter a man-made sanctuary that was only a copy [*antitypos:* "copy, antitype, representation"] of the true one. (Heb 9:24)

> The law is only a shadow [*skia:* shadow, in contrast to reality] of the good things that are coming—not the realities themselves. (Heb 10:1)

> [Abraham] was looking forward to the city with foundations, whose architect and builder is God. (Heb 11:10)

> God . . . has prepared [*hētoimasen:* aor. *hetoimazō*, "make ready"] a city for them. (Heb 11:16)

> You have come to . . . the heavenly Jerusalem, the city of the living God. (Heb 12:22)

> Here we do not have an enduring city, but we are looking for the city that is to come. (Heb 13:14)

> I saw the Holy City, the new Jerusalem, coming down out of heaven from God. (Rev 21:2)

On the basis of these New Testament witnesses, I would like to challenge three prevalent assumptions about "heaven" (= new Jerusalem = Jerusalem above = new creation) in the minds of many Christians today: (1) heaven is only *future*, (2) heaven is only *spiritual*, and (3) heaven is *inaccessible*. I believe that all three assumptions are faulty and out of accord with the teachings of Scripture.

The more correct understanding of the preceding texts is that heaven or the new Jerusalem (= new creation) already *exists* in the unseen dimensions but will be *visibly* revealed when Christ returns visibly and in a physical, bodily form at the end of history. The writer of Hebrews informs us that in true worship we have *already* arrived at the heavenly Zion/Jerusalem (Heb 12:22), as truly as the Israelites in the old covenant had arrived at the visible Mount Sinai. The John of Revelation sees the new Jerusalem coming down of out heaven from God; he sees a city already fully built, not just bricks and mortar arriving on semitrailers for some future completion date. The transition is not from not-existing city to existing city, but from invisible, existing city to *visible* and existing city.

The second pervasive popular misunderstanding of the "metaphysics" of heaven is that heaven is purely spiritual, consisting of disembodied spirits flying around in some gaseous and ethereal realm. Let us be very clear about this: *this notion of heaven is gnostic and Neo-Platonic and a heretical distortion of biblical teaching.* Strong language, to be sure, but I believe that it is justified. Neo-Platonism, which rooted itself in the Christian church and spirituality from the time of Pseudo-Dionysius in the sixth century A.D, presupposed an alien vision of salvation and the spiritual life as a flight from matter and the body to the pure realm of spirit, away from the changing world of distinctions into the changeless world of the One.[11] Heaven is depicted as a *city:* a structured environment, a complex topography that in some sense has extension and dimensionality, and is occupied by bodies located in some form of space.

Biblical spirituality and salvation is not a rising from the world of matter to a realm of pure, disembodied spirit, but rather a transition from matter "under the curse" to a redeemed and *glorified* material creation ("creation itself will be liberated from its bondage to decay and brought into the glorious freedom of the children of God" [Rom 8:21]). The inaugurated eschatology of the New Testament teaches not a transition from matter to pure spirit but rather from matter in its present state to "matter enhanced" and glorified, suffused with the glorious Spirit of God, who was present to the material creation (Gen 1:2) and has never abandoned it (cf. Ps 104:30, presence of the life-giving Spirit in the biological world).[12]

In his recent study of heaven and the new creation, N. T. Wright has emphatically underscored the radical difference between any form of Gnostic "heaven" and the biblical vision. The biblical new creation "is the ultimate rejection of all types of Gnosticism, of every worldview that sees the final separation of the world from God, of the physical from the spiritual, of earth from heaven."[13] As Wright notes, it [Rev 21–22] is "not we who go to heaven; it is heaven that comes to earth."[14]

---

[11]For a concise and insightful account of how Neo-Platonism was imported into Christian spirituality, and its pervasive influence, see Evelyn Underhill, "A Historical Sketch of European Mysticism from the Beginning of the Christian Era to the Death of William Blake," in *Mysticism: A Study in the Nature and Development of Man's Spiritual Consciousness* (New York: Meridian Books, 1955), pp. 453-473; esp. pp. 456-57, 459, 463, 466. For the sense of alienation from the material world in Gnosticism, see Hans Jonas, *The Gnostic Religion* (Boston: Beacon Press, 1958), esp. pp. 250-53.

[12]Jürgen Moltmann has called fresh attention to the work and presence of the Spirit in creation and its implications for ecological theology (*The Spirit of Life: A Universal Affirmation* [Minneapolis: Fortress, 1992]).

[13]N. T. Wright, *Surprised by Hope: Rethinking Heaven, the Resurrection, and the Mission of the Church* (New York: HarperOne, 2008), p. 104.

[14]Ibid.

In the third place, we need to rethink the common assumption that the reality of heaven and the new Jerusalem is *inaccessible*—that the heavenly reality will be experienced only in the future, "when we die and go to heaven." This is not the assumption of Paul and of the writer of Hebrews. In true worship we are already in the presence of the new Jerusalem, of God, the risen Christ, the angels and the saints and martyrs (Heb 12:22-25); we can already experience the powers of the age to come (Heb 6:5). If we but have the eyes to see it, every Sunday morning we are "in the presence of the angels" and all the heavenly host.[15] We are really present to heaven, and heaven is really present to us—again, the reality of *inaugurated* eschatology.

The very practical point that should not be missed in this claim that the reality of heaven is now in some sense "accessible" to the church on earth is that the very *transformative energy* of the age to come ("the powers of the coming age" [Heb 6:5]) is *already* being made available to the church for its ministry and mission. Alas, all too often the church today is being run on the natural energies of *this age*, rather than the supernatural energy loosed by the resurrection of Jesus and the descent of the Spirit! If we have lost our heavenly imagination, we will be disinclined to access, by faith and prayer, the heavenly energy from above.[16] Which energy does your church run on?

Paul reminds us that we are *already* in heaven, seated with Christ in the heavenly places (Eph 2:6). Our molecular selves are still very much located on earth, but since we are united to Christ, with our spirits connected to Christ by the Holy Spirit (1 Cor 6:17), our extended selves are projected (Skyped) and represented in heaven by the Holy Spirit. As Calvin rightly observed, "the Spirit truly unites things separated by space."[17]

---

[15]The presence of the heavenly worship to the church on earth is reflected in the words of the eucharistic liturgy, "Therefore with Angels and Archangels, and with all the company of heaven, we laud and magnify thy glorious Name; evermore praising thee, and saying, Holy, Holy, Holy, Lord God of hosts, Heaven and earth are full of thy glory: Glory be to thee, O Lord Most High" (*Book of Common Prayer* [New York: Church Pension Fund, 1945], p. 77). This *Sanctus*, rooted in Isaiah 6 and Jewish liturgy, became an acclamation of the people from the time of the fourth century. See Marion J. Hatchett, *Commentary on the American Prayer Book* (New York: HarperCollins, 1995), p. 363.

[16]The term *divine energy* is not used to imply that the Holy Spirit is an *impersonal* force like electricity or some New Age spirit; rather, the Holy Spirit is a divine person who personally brings the energy of God (*dunamis*) to the church and to the believer.

[17]John Calvin, *Institutes of the Christian Religion*, 4.17.10.

By now you may be saying, "This is all well and good—or perhaps it is well and good—but I still have trouble getting my mind around what Paul and John and the writer to the Hebrews seem to be saying. It still seems unreal to me." Fair enough. I believe that the problem is that the modern post-Copernican, Newtonian view of the universe ushered in by the scientific revolution of the seventeenth century, and economies of material abundance and entertainment, have made it difficult for modern Christians to take the biblical heaven seriously. "Where is heaven, anyway? Six trillion light-years from earth? If heaven is a place, where is it located in our modern cosmological models? Where is 'up there' anyway? And our material needs have been so well supplied by our consumer society that we no longer need 'pie in the sky by and by.'"

Modern science teaches us (or is thought to teach us) that the paradigm of the *real* is primarily (if not exclusively) that which is *visible* and *material* in nature and measurable by the scientific method. Reality is constituted by visible, material particles in motion, and Paul and John's heaven or new creation don't seem to qualify as real by these criteria. As a result, for quite some time heaven has been fading from Christian preaching and from the Christian consciousness and imagination generally.[18]

In concluding this section I would like to suggest that if the world of Newtonian science tended to close down the Christian imagination, there are some developments in recent science and cosmology that can actually help to open it up and create some cognitive and imaginative space for the biblical heaven and new creation. The notions that I have in mind are those of *dark matter* and *hyperspace*. These developments show that the Newtonian, Enlightenment picture of the universe is now seriously out of date, and that it is at least possible to imagine and conceptualize heaven in new ways.

---

[18]On the history of various notions of heaven in church history and Western civilization, see Colleen McDannell and Bernard Lang, *Heaven: A History* (New Haven, Conn: Yale University Press, 1988), with general summary on pp. 353-58; Alister E. McGrath, *A Brief History of Heaven* (Oxford: Blackwell, 2003); Jerry L. Walls, *Heaven: The Logic of Eternal Joy* (New York: Oxford University Press, 2002), pp. 3-9. The eclipse of heaven in the modern world is documented in A. J. Conyers, *The Loss of Transcendence and Its Effect on Modern Life* (South Bend, Ind.: St. Augustine's Press, 1999). Conyers believes that for many moderns heaven "has become little more than a caricature, conjuring up the saints and angels of baroque frescoes . . . in the church only a hint remains of the power it once exercised in the hearts of believers" (ibid., p. 11).

Scientists now believe that as much as 80 percent of the matter in the known universe is "dark matter," with ordinary matter making up only about 20 percent.[19] This dark matter, which is thought to be a possible explanation for anomalies in the observed rotation of galaxies, is "dark" in that it does not appear in the visible light range and does not interact in the usual ways with ordinary matter. So what does this have to do with a discussion of the eclipse of heaven? Simply this: current science reminds us that only a small part of physical reality is directly observable with our human senses. The "real" is not limited to that which is *visible* to the un-aided human eye; much of the real is detectable only with sophisticated scientific instrumentation that can extend the reach of the human senses.

I have never seen a black hole, but I believe that there are good reasons to believe they actually exist. Indeed, even *ordinary* forms of energy—radio waves, ultraviolet, infrared, gamma rays and so forth—lie outside the visible light range of the electromagnetic spectrum. The fact that my eyes cannot see into the infrared does not prove that in-frared radiation does not exist; if my eyes are enhanced with night-vision goggles, I can then see objects that are otherwise invisible.

The point is that our commonsense notions of the real are biased in favor of the molecular objects (rocks, trees, cats, dogs, etc.) that appear in the visible light range, but our human eyes detect only a small slice of what's really out there. The commonsense view of the world is as much a commentary on the limits of our human physiology as it is on the boundaries of the real.

The conservative Old Testament scholar Meredith G. Kline has ac-tually invoked the analogy of dark matter in his discussion of the "two-register cosmology" of Genesis and the Bible, an "upper register" (in-visible but real) of heaven, and a "lower register" of the visible earth. While the upper register of heaven, where God and the angels dwell, is invisible prior to the consummation, it is "not to be thought of as oc-cupying a separate place off at a distance from the earth or outside the cosmos," according to Kline. "Heaven and earth relate to each other spatially more after the manner of . . . dark matter and visible matter.

---

[19]Richard Panek, *The 4 Percent Universe: Dark Matter, Dark Energy, and the Race to Discover the Rest of Reality* (New York: Houghton Mifflin, 2011), p. 116..

When earthlings experience a proleptic opening of their eyes, they see that the very spot where they are standing is the gate of heaven (Gen. 28:16-17), filled with heavenly chariots of fire (2 Kgs. 6:17)."[20] Just as dark matter, though invisible, is thought to interpenetrate the visible universe, so could we conceive of a subtle matter of the heavenly world interpenetrating it as well.

Consider also the mathematical analogy of *hyperspace*, or higher-dimensional spaces. Since its original publication in 1884, Edwin Abbott's *Flatland*, a story of the inhabitants of two-dimensional world visited by beings from a three-space world, has fascinated generations of mathematicians and ordinary readers.[21] The two-dimensional inhabitants of Flatland (circles, squares, triangles, etc.) are mystified when a sphere passes through their world, appearing first as a point, then a gradually increasing circle, then diminishing again to a point, and then disappearing.

This transcends their normal two-dimensional world, and they find it impossible to imagine a world of three dimensions and three-dimensional objects. Even though their two-dimensional world is actually embedded in a three-dimensional space, they cannot see into that third dimension and it seems unreal to their imagination. *If* our three-dimensional spatial world were embedded in a *four*-dimensional space, an object (such as the body of the ascended Christ) would be invisible from the perspective of our three-dimensional universe. On such a view, Christ "ascended into the fourth dimension"; heaven could exist in a higher dimension of the universe.[22]

"All of this is very speculative," you might be saying. Well, yes and no: there is some empirical evidence, though indirect, for the existence of dark matter, and the concept of four (and higher-dimensional) spaces is well accepted by mathematicians and used in current physical and cosmological theories.[23] Analogies are analogies and not strict arguments, of course; but

[20]Meredith G. Kline, "Space and Time in the Genesis Cosmogony," *Perspectives on Science and Christian Faith* 48 (1996): 2.

[21]For a critical edition with notes and bibliography, see Edwin A. Abbott, *Flatland*, ed. William F. Lindgren and Thomas F. Banchoff (Cambridge: Cambridge University Press, 2010).

[22]Cf. the suggestion of Thomas F. Torrance that Christ's ascension "higher than *all* the heavens" (Eph 4:10) implies a movement beyond the space-time manifold of our known world (*Space, Time, and Resurrection* [Grand Rapids: Eerdmans, 1976], pp. 128-31).

[23]On higher-dimensional spaces, see Rudy Rucker, *The Fourth Dimension: Toward a Geometry of Higher Reality* (Boston: Houghton Mifflin, 1984); and Michio Kaku, *Hyperspace: A Scientific*

the point is that such notions as dark matter and higher-dimensional spaces remind us that the *real* is not limited to the *visible*. Such analogies open up *conceptual space* within which we can ponder the biblical reality of heaven and the world to come, and at the same time not reject modern scientific understandings of the physical universe that God has created.

PRACTICAL APPLICATION

Try a whole-brain meditation exercise (see section two in chap. 6), spending thirty minutes or so prayerfully pondering two texts: Colossians 3:1-3 ("set your hearts on things above"), and Revelation 21–22, the new Jerusalem (since you are "seated with [Christ] in the heavenly realms" [Eph 2:6]). Picture yourself *inside* the new Jerusalem, in the presence of the risen Christ; reflect on the splendor and beauty of the new creation, and its *immensity* (a cube 1,400 miles on each side! [Rev 21:16]); reflect on this revealed image of a *new reality* that is the current creation enhanced immeasurably in its "intensity, immensity, density, and beauty"; thank God in prayer that you have been chosen from eternity (Eph 1:4) to enjoy communion with the triune God forever and increasingly in this new creation.

ANTHROPOLOGY
Who Am I? Christian as Trinitarian-Ecclesial Self

Anthropology is being used here as a technical term in theology to refer to the biblical and Christian understanding of the human person. Who

---

Odyssey Through Parallel Universes, Time Warps, and the Tenth Dimension (New York: Oxford University Press, 1994). Physicists seeking to unify the law of gravity (General Relativity) with the laws of quantum mechanics are working with "string theories" that postulate the existence of ten dimensions. See Brian Greene, "More Dimensions Than Meet the Eye," chap. 8 in *The Elegant Universe: Superstrings, Hidden Dimensions, and the Quest for the Ultimate Theory* (New York: Vintage Books, 1999). In string theory "extradimensional geometry determines fundamental physical attributes like particle mass and charge that we observe in the usual three large space dimensions of common experience" (ibid., p. 206).

are we? How do we understand our fundamental identity and purpose in life as we approach the Scriptures in prayerful meditation? Our sense of personal identity, either conscious or unconsciously presupposed, does influence the way that we approach texts. If I am looking at a set of papers and hearing my friend explain her family tree and the fruits of her genealogical research, I may listen with polite and sincere interest; if someone shows me surprising new information about *my* family tree—that I am descended from some great celebrity from the past—then my interest is even deeper!

The Bible is, in a very real sense, my "family tree." I read the biblical text not as outsider but as insider. Jesus Christ, the central character in the entire biblical narrative, is not a stranger to me but—by virtue of my union with him—is *my* ancestor, *my* brother and *my* beloved friend. "My lover is mine and I am his. . . . His banner over me is love" (Song 2:16, 4).

The words of Jesus, and the words of Scripture generally, have as their highest purpose the sharing with us the joy that Jesus experienced in his own loving relationship with the Father: "I say these things while I am still in the world, so that *they may have the full measure of my joy within them*" (Jn 17:13, emphasis added). The words of divine revelation are given to us and to the church for a variety of purposes: *information* (knowledge about God) and *formation* (being changed by God), but the deepest and highest purpose of divine revelation is to *enjoy communion with* God—participating in increasing measure in the joyous, loving experience of Jesus' communion with the Father, in the fellowship of the Holy Spirit.

Because I am united to Christ, I am also united to the Father, to the Holy Spirit and to the other members of the body of Christ; my core identity is that of a trinitarian-ecclesial self. Upon my conversion I am incorporated by the Holy Spirit into the body of Christ (1 Cor 12:13), and I am more truly, deeply and permanently networked and "friended" to the Father, Son and Holy Spirit, and to other believers in the church than I am to my "friends" on Facebook. The Holy Spirit is like a wireless, broadband connection to the triune God—although so much more—and to the communion of saints in the heavenly realms. So, then, because I am in Christ, I am a new creation (2 Cor 5:17). My old ways of defining myself, my old identity based on gender, class, ethnicity, nationality or occupation (cf. in Christ "there is neither Jew nor Greek, slave nor free, male nor female" [Gal 3:28]) have been superseded by the new reality, the new ontology ushered in by the incarnation, death, resurrection and ascension of the Son of God and by the coming of the Holy Spirit. I need to reprogram my mind and think of myself in a radically new way, as one whose true identity and reality is found in *relationship* to the persons of the Holy Trinity and to persons of the body of Christ, the family of God. One of the purposes and benefits of biblical meditation is to help us grow more deeply and more experientially into this new identity of who we really are in Christ.

This new self, this new identity—as trinitarian-ecclesial self—distinguishes Christian identity from the ways in which personal identity is understood in other world religions and philosophies. The Vedanta tradition in Hinduism tells me that my true identity is found in understanding and experiencing the truth of the equation "Atman (self) = Brahman": not union with Christ but union with the impersonal Absolute. The Buddha tells me that the whole notion of a permanent "self" is a delusion I must be liberated from; the real story is anatta or "no-self"; the final destination is not communion with the triune God but that of a nirvana or sunyata ("emptiness") beyond knowledge and all conceptual distinctions. Christianity, like Hinduism and Buddhism, recognizes the critical distinction between the empirical (common-sense) self and the true self, but understands this distinction in a fundamentally different (trinitarian-ecclesial) way.

The Enlightenment self of modernity tells me that who I really am is defined by money, sex, power and natural selection. According to Karl Marx I am *Homo economicus*, a creature determined by money, industrial capitalism, class interest and the means of production. Sigmund Freud would have me believe that my true identity is rooted in my hidden sexual drives and "death instinct." Friedrich Nietzsche and his "hermeneutics of suspicion" tells me that my deepest motivations, deeper than all my supposed religious or philosophical beliefs, involve the "will to power" and the desire to dominate other people. Darwin tells me that, at the end of the day, I should think of myself as a highly evolved primate, the unintended consequence of a very long process of undirected natural selection.

Theorists of postmodernity would have me believe that the only self to be had is a socially constructed self, a "do-it-yourself" identity that you cobble together for yourself as best you can and change whenever you wish.[24] "All the world is a stage," and I can represent myself to others on Facebook just as I choose to do so, limited only by my own imagination (and, very minimally, by the network police).

Both the modern and postmodern selves are autonomous, thinking, acting and defining themselves independently, apart from lasting, fundamental accountability to God and to others. Both the modern and postmodern selves are locked into the *individualism* so characteristic of our culture, and do not offer the resources to get beyond it. The Christian view of the self, on the other hand—the trinitarian-ecclesial self—sees personal identity as one in which we act in partnership and cooperation with God the Father, Son and Holy Spirit, and in partnership with other Christians. We read the Bible in partnership with the great tradition, not intending to read our private meanings into the text but having a due regard for what the Holy Spirit has taught the people of God over the centuries of church history.

In chapter three, in the section on "Union with Christ," the biblical and theological dimensions of this pivotal concept have already been discussed, and in the excursus, "How Personal Agents Are Located in Space," the concept of the "extended self" was introduced to further explicate the nature of this union. We are truly bonded to Christ by the Holy Spirit ("He who unites himself with the Lord is one with him in spirit" [1 Cor 6:17]; "we were all baptized by one Spirit into one body" [1 Cor 12:13]). Union with Christ is real—not just a metaphor—

---

[24]On the social construction of the self in a postmodern, media-saturated context, see Walter Truett Anderson, "Being Someone: The Construction of Personal Reality," chap. 6 in *Reality Isn't What It Used to Be* (New York: HarperCollins, 1990); Kenneth J. Gergen, *The Saturated Self: Dilemmas of Identity in Contemporary Life* (New York: Basic Books, 1991); Kenneth J. Gergen, *The Social Construction of the Person* (New York: Springer-Verlag, 1985); Thomas de Zengotita, *Mediated: How the Media Shapes Your World and the Way You Live In It* (New York: Bloomsbury, 2005), esp. chaps. 4-5. "The new superficiality, the surface quality of ubiquitous representation. . . . You become an elaborate apparatus of evolving shtick that you deploy improvisationally as circumstances warrant . . . overscheduled busyness . . . living in a flood of surfaces. . . . [O]ur representational technologies have colonized our minds. . . . [O]ur thoughts no longer wander on their own, stocked only with materials drawn from direct experience" (Zengotita, *Mediated*, pp. 186, 187, 189, 196).

because the Holy Spirit is real and the relationship that I have with Christ established by the Holy Spirit is real and enduring.

The Holy Spirit connects and extends my spirit to Christ, and the Spirit extends the heart and mind of Christ into my mind and heart. The Holy Spirit connects me to the risen Christ so that I am truly "seated with [Christ] in the heavenly realms" (Eph 2:6) by faith—during worship and during Christ-centered, faithful meditation on Scripture.

I would now like to further explicate the concepts of union with Christ and the "extended self" with the help of J. A. Austin's notion of "performative utterances" and John Searle's theory of the "construction of social realities." This will help us to better understand how such Pauline expressions as being "in Christ" or "crucified with Christ" or "risen with Christ" can be more than figures of speech, but rather descriptions of a new and real state of affairs—new facts in the universe, so to speak.

Austin, in his widely read book *How to Do Things with Words*, pointed out that language not only conveys information and makes assertions, but also "does things" or makes things happen.[25] Under the right circumstances, saying certain things brings a new reality into being. For example, when a minister says the words, "I now declare you to be husband and wife," a new social fact has been brought into being: two human beings really are married and to be recognized by society in their new relationship, with its rights and obligations.

John Searle has extended this insight about the nature of language with his theory of the "construction of social reality."[26] For Searle, the category of the real is constituted not only by natural facts and objects, such as sticks and stones, but also by social facts, such as laws, institutions, money, the economy and so forth. Social facts, unlike natural facts, are created by human mind and intentionality, but once they have been created, they have an objective social existence that is not necessarily limited to the intention of the creator.

---

[25]J. L. Austin, *How to Do Things with Words* (Oxford: Clarendon, 1962).

[26]John Searle, "The Structure of the Social Universe: How the Mind Creates an Objective Social Reality," and "How Language Works: Speech as a Kind of Human Action," chaps. 5-6 in *Mind, Language and Society: Philosophy in the Real World* (New York: Basic Books, 1998); John Searle, *The Construction of Social Reality* (New York: Free Press, 1995).

Social facts are *ontologically* subjective, but *socially* objective. For example, consider the case of our paper money. There is no inherent reason that a piece of paper printed by the U.S. Treasury with the picture of Abraham Lincoln on it should be worth five dollars—but once created and defined as such by competent authority it *really is* five dollars, at least in a certain context: within the national boundaries of the United States.

Searle's theory of the construction of social realities can be distilled in the following rule or principle: "A new social fact is created when a competent authority declares that 'X counts as Y in context Z.'" In the case of money, the U.S. Treasury declares that this piece of paper with the picture of Abraham Lincoln shall count as five dollars in the context of the United States economy and legal system. In the case of the marriage ceremony, the minister's words "I hereby declare . . . " count as the creation of a marriage relationship in the context of American law and religious tradition.

The reader may have already guessed how Searle's theory can be extended, analogically, within the context of a biblical worldview to support a theory of the "divine construction of spiritual realities." God's powerful, sovereign and creative words are the ultimate performative utterances. When God says "Let there be light," light is created and there are new facts in the universe. When God, the ultimate competent authority, says in his Word, the Bible, that in the context of the church and of Christian faith, my baptism counts as my being united with Christ in his death and resurrection (Rom 6:4), then it is really so: I really have died and risen with Christ. Because of my God-declared union with Christ, I indeed truly have a new identity, even more deeply and lastingly true than the new identity as a married man declared by a human minister.

The God of Abraham, who can give life to the dead, and who "calls things that are not [yet existing] as though they are" (Rom 4:17), creates new facts on the ground by the very power of his Word. When he says to Abraham, "I have made you the father of many nations," then this is true in the sight of God and by the reality of the *promise*, which, ontologically is a more powerful and determinative reality than the biological and molecular facts of the barrenness of Sarah's womb.

The power of performative utterances and creation of new social facts can also be illustrated by the process of becoming a citizen. When the official of the U.S. Immigration Service leads the candidates for citizenship in the pledge of allegiance, all legal requirements and preconditions having been satisfied, and says, "I now declare that you are citizens of the United States of America"—the person in question is no longer a Mexican or a Peruvian, but an American citizen, with a new personal identity, who can identify with the core stories of the American experience: George Washington at Valley Forge, Martin Luther King Jr.'s "I Have a Dream" speech and so forth.

When God's Word says that, as a consequence of my union with Christ, my citizenship is in heaven (Phil 3:20), then it is a fact that my citizenship is in heaven, and my identity in Christ becomes more fundamental than my identity as an American. All the stories of the Bible, from Genesis to Revelation—the biblical metanarrative—become my stories, the big story within which I understand my personal story as a Christian, as a new trinitarian-ecclesial self and member of the body of Christ. As I meditate on the Scriptures in faith, those stories become more and more my own, gradually transforming the way that I see myself, God, and the world.

TELEOLOGY AND SOTERIOLOGY
The Purpose and Fulfillment of Human Life

Teleology (Greek *telos,* "end, goal, purpose") refers to a concept or philosophy of the meaning and purpose of human life, and *soteriology* (Greek *sōtēr,* "savior") is the technical term in theology for the doctrine of salvation. A state of salvation is a state in which humans experience ultimate and final fulfillment, and implies that the true purpose and meaning of human life has been achieved. Just as it is important to have a clear picture of the final destination before you pull out of the driveway for a family vacation, so it is very important to have a clear vision of the basic purpose of human life and of its fulfillment as we read the Scriptures and serve God in the church and the world.

I can think of no finer or more succinct statement of the meaning and purpose of human life than that which is stated in the very first question and answer of the Westminster Shorter Catechism:

Q.1. What is the chief end of man?
A. Man's chief end is to glorify God, and to enjoy him forever.

This is a profound statement, deeply rooted in the truth of the Scriptures, and upon which we do well to ponder and meditate. Human life is to be centered in God, not the self; and human life finds its fulfillment not apart from God but in right relationship to God. The highest purpose for which humans were created is to glorify God in worship and life obedience, and to enjoy God in those very acts of worship and obedience.[27]

What does it mean to glorify God? The answer in the Children's Catechism (based on the Shorter Catechism) is a good and biblical one: We glorify God "by loving him and doing what he commands." We express our love for God in corporate worship and private prayer and meditation as we offer up ourselves to God in acts of adoration, praise and thanksgiving.

In expressing our love for God in this way, we are fulfilling the highest purpose for which we are created. God, speaking through the prophet Isaiah, speaks of his redeemed people:

Everyone who is called by my name,
        whom I created for my glory . . .
the people I formed for myself,
        that they may proclaim my praise. (Is 43:7, 21, emphasis added)

In the magnificent opening doxological section of Ephesians 1:3-14, the apostle Paul, his mind and heart filled with gratitude and praise, declares that the end and purpose of God's redemption in Christ was that we "might be for the praise of his glory" (v. 12). To be in right relationship to God is to experience joy in God; in his farewell discourse Jesus taught the disciples that "I say these things while I am still in the

---

[27]For the theme of finding true enjoyment in God, see John Piper, *Desiring God: Meditations of a Christian Hedonist* (Sisters, Ore.: Multnomah Books, 1996).

world *so that they may have the full measure of my joy within them"* (Jn 17:13, emphasis added).

These texts remind us that the worship of God and the enjoyment of God in worship and meditation are not merely *instrumental* goods but *intrinsic* goods. Being in the presence of the God who loves us intensely is the Christian's highest joy and pleasure. While it is instrumentally good in that it energizes us for service and mission, this enjoyment of God is good in itself, for it is indeed the realization of the highest purpose for which we were made.

If enjoying God and being in the presence of God is the highest purpose for which I exist, then worship and biblical meditation are not low priorities but high priorities; they are worthy of my best time, energy and focused attention. Keeping this highest purpose of human existence—joyful communion with God—clearly in mind should be an excellent motivator for our meditative practice.

Salvation is the fulfillment of human existence, the fulfillment of humanity's highest purpose and goal. As such, one's understanding of salvation (soteriology) is inherently and logically connected to one's understanding of theology (the ultimately real) and anthropology (the nature and purpose of the self or human). One could, in fact, define salvation as a state in which *the true self is rightly related to ultimate reality*, enjoying loving communion with Father, Son and Holy Spirit.

The different world religions have very different concepts of salvation, because they have fundamentally different understandings of the "true self" and of "ultimate reality."[28] The Christian understanding of salvation is deeply and fundamentally trinitarian in nature, as we have already noted earlier (see "Trinitarian God, Christian Meditation"). Salvation is not just "going to heaven when I die," though it is indeed that, but rather our participation, beginning now, in the joy that Jesus the beloved Son experiences in being loved by his (and our) heavenly Father, by and in fellowship with the Holy Spirit. My sal-

---

[28]As noted earlier, for Buddhism, there is no unchanging, eternal "true self" or "soul" in the Christian sense of the term, and the Buddhist nirvana is radically different from the Christian heaven or new creation. On the pluralism of concepts of salvation in the world religions, see Mark Heim, *Salvations: Truth and Difference in Religion* (Maryknoll, N.Y.: Orbis, 1995).

vation means "being glorified with the glory of God" and enjoying a close, personal communion with all three persons of the Trinity: Father, Son and Holy Spirit. We "turn our eyes upon Jesus," but also upon the Father and the Holy Spirit.

This focus on the three persons of the Trinity, persons eternally and essentially connected in holy, loving relationships, can help us to stand against the individualism of our culture and Lone Ranger styles of ministry in the church. I have been saved by grace alone, but I have not been saved alone or to be alone; we have been saved for community, for communion and union with God and for communion with the body of Christ.

The nature of Christian salvation could even be stated this way: *Enjoying in fullness the joyful communion of joyful communities.* Since the meaning of this statement may not be self-evident, allow me to unpack it a bit. Being in God's presence as a redeemed person is the highest joy that a human being can experience:

> You will fill me with joy in your presence,
>> with eternal pleasures at your right hand. . . .
> They feast on the abundance of your house;
>> you give them drink from your river of delights. (Ps 16:11; 36:8)

The triune God, Father, Son and Holy Spirit, is a joyous community of persons who enjoy infinite delight, happiness and pleasure in one another's company; our salvation consists in being invited into that gloriously happy and joyous fellowship.[29] God's purpose in redemption is to make the church, his body and his people, a joyous community of persons who are filled to the full with the love and joy of God ("that they may have the *full measure* of *my joy* within them" [Jn 17:13]; "his body, the *fullness* of him who fills everything in every way" [Eph 1:23]; "that you may be filled to the measure of *all the fullness of God*" [Eph 3:19, emphasis added]).

---

[29]Theologically, we can recognize that joy is an eternal, *intrinsic* attribute of God's being, while wrath is, technically, an *accidental* property in consequence of human sin. Wrath is not intrinsic to the being of God in the same way that joy is. God was not wrathful before sin entered the universe, and God could have chosen to create a universe where sin would not exist; sin does not exist necessarily, and consequently neither does the wrath of God. This distinction can be very important at the existential level for how we view God; unfortunately, many Christians have a view of God in which wrath is more fundamental than joy!

The church is a joyful community in communion with the joyful community of the triune God. Father, Son and Holy Spirit are not only infinitely happy in themselves but also gloriously delighted to have *us as redeemed people in their presence*. The prophet Zephaniah, in one of the most remarkable statements in all Scripture, and one vitally important for our own images and vision of salvation, portrays God as singing with delight over his beloved children:

> The Lord your God is with you [real presence],
> > he is mighty to save [real power];
> He will take *great delight in you* [real joy],
> > he will quiet you with his love [real peace],
> > he will rejoice over you with singing. (Zeph 3:17, emphasis added)[30]

Our joyful songs of gratitude in worship reflect back to God his own joyful and exuberant singing over his people, expressing his heartfelt delight in having us in his presence. Such is the glorious vision of salvation that can deepen our experience of delight in God and enrich our meditation on Scripture.

PRACTICAL APPLICATION

Reflect for a while on the following texts: Zephaniah 3:17 (God singing with delight over his people); Luke 15:20 (the Father's joy at the return of his prodigal son); Romans 5:5 (God's love poured into our hearts by the Holy Spirit). Reflect on the fact that God takes joy in you, his beloved son or daughter; picture yourself as being joyfully welcomed home and embraced by your dear *Abba* Father—and rejoice!

---

[30]This text, I believe, is the only text in the Bible that portrays God as *singing*. God's singing is a fitting expression of the joy, harmony and beauty that is intrinsic to God's being. We can well imagine that from all eternity Father, Son and Holy Spirit, eternally loving, have not only been speaking to one another but singing to one another as well!

5

A New Way of Knowing God and Reading the Bible

Seeing into Heaven Now

〰
〰

EPISTEMOLOGY
Knowing God and Heaven by Word and Spirit

Epistemology is the technical term in philosophy for the theory of knowledge. Epistemology, which is concerned with the nature of knowledge and truth claims, and the grounds upon which such claims are justified, seeks to provide answers to such questions as: What does it mean to know something? How is knowledge different from belief and opinion? On what ground or grounds is some claim to be justified as genuine knowledge? Epistemology has been a major preoccupation of modern philosophers in the wake of the scientific revolution of the seventeenth century and the work of Enlightenment thinkers such as René Descartes, John Locke, David Hume and Immanuel Kant, who challenged in various ways the religiously based theories of knowledge that had been the basis of Western civilization during the period of Christendom.[1]

---

[1]For a concise survey of the history of (Western) epistemology see D. W. Hamlyn, "Epistemology, History of," in *The Encyclopedia of Philosophy*, ed. Paul Edwards (New York: Macmillan, 1967), 3:8-38; on the history of theories of knowledge in Buddhism see David J. Kalupahana, *A History of Buddhist Philosophy: Continuities and Discontinuities* (Honolulu: University of Hawaii Press, 1992); on Indian and Buddhist epistemological thought see Ninian Smart, *Doctrine and Argument in Indian Philosophy* (London: George Allen & Unwin, 1964); on current trends in modern Western epistemology see David L. Wolfe, *Epistemology* (Downers Grove, Ill.: InterVarsity Press, 1983).

The purpose in this section is not to give a comprehensive discussion of the topic but only to indicate how the elements of a biblical worldview that we have been discussing—inaugurated eschatology, union with Christ, the Trinity, anthropology and so forth—inform a Christian understanding of epistemology, and how such a biblical epistemology can support and enrich our meditation on Scripture.

The basic premise of this section is that the inaugurated eschatology of the New Testament—the new reality that the powers of the age to come have already arrived in the church because of the resurrection of Jesus Christ and the outpouring of the Spirit (Heb 6:5)—implies a new inaugurated epistemology that is different from the old epistemologies of "this age," the old age that is already passing away. Because of the resurrection of Jesus and the arrival of the Spirit, fundamental questions such as, What types of things exist? and How do we know them? cannot simply be answered in the same old ways. A new ontology demands a new epistemology.

The proposal here is that we need to recognize an inaugurated epistemology in Paul, a *logopneumatic* (Word and Spirit) theory of knowledge that had its origins in the apostle's encounter with the risen Christ on the Damascus road and his own personal reception of the Spirit (Acts 9:17-18). Because of these life-changing experiences, Paul knew that he himself was a new creation (2 Cor 5:17) and that his mind had been transformed to look at the world in a fundamentally new way (cf. Rom 12:2).

Paul's transformed theory of knowledge that I am calling a logopneumatic doctrine, because of the central roles played in it by revealed words of God and the Holy Spirit, transcends the limits of theories of knowledge of this age, which could be described by the terms *empiricism* and *rationalism*. By empiricism I mean a theory of knowledge that holds that the primary (or exclusive) basis of knowledge of the real world external to the human mind is sense experience. By rationalism I mean a theory of knowledge that holds that the foundations of knowledge (if such foundations exist) are to be found in reason, logic and clear ideas.[2]

---

[2]In the history of Western philosophy, generally speaking, Aristotle, Locke and Hume would be seen as standing in the empirical tradition, and Plato, Descartes and Hegel in the tradition

Paul would recognize that the sensible things of this world (for example, "The sun is shining today") are indeed knowable by sense experience, and that some propositions are established by logical argument (for example, "If the dead are not raised, then Christ has not been raised either" [1 Cor 15:16]). But Paul would deny that sense experience and reason *exhaust* the possible sources of knowledge; he knew that God's words of divine revelation and the Spirit of God are sources of knowledge about the invisible realities of God, salvation, heaven, eternal life and the world to come. If in fact there are realities that truly exist, and that are not detectable by sense experience or unaided human reason alone, then neither empiricism nor rationalism would be adequate to recognize these ontological facts. An enlarged epistemology would be needed.

It is not difficult to demonstrate the apostle's logopneumatic epistemology from his writings. A good point of departure is the text in 1 Corinthians 2:9-14, where Paul is contrasting the divinely revealed origins of the gospel as the wisdom of God with the worldly wisdom of human philosophy:

As it is written,

"No eye has seen,
        no ear has heard,
no mind has conceived,
        what God has prepared for those who love him" [Is 64:4]—

but God has revealed it to us by his Spirit.

The Spirit searches all things, even the deep things of God. . . . [N]o one knows the thoughts of God except the Spirit of God. We have not received the spirit of the world but the Spirit who is from God, *that we may understand what God has freely given us.* [emphasis added] This is what we speak, not in words taught by human wisdom but in words taught by the Spirit, expressing spiritual truths in spiritual words. The man without the Spirit does not accept the things that come from the Spirit of God, for they are foolishness to him, and he cannot understand them, because they are spiritually discerned.

---

of rationalism or idealism. Kant attempted to integrate these traditions in his "transcendental" and "critical" theory of knowledge.

For Paul, the gospel, the wisdom of God, is beyond the reach of empiricism ("no eye has seen, no ear has heard") and rationalism ("no mind has conceived"). There is a principle at work here that "like is known by like." The things of physical sense are known by the physical senses; the things of logic and mathematics are known by logic and mathematics; but the things that are ontologically *spirit* (the mind of God, words of God, the content of the gospel) must be known by the Spirit ("God has revealed it to us by his Spirit" [v. 10]).

The Holy Spirit reveals the words from the mind of God, searching the very depths of the divine being (v. 10), and *illuminates* these words to our human understanding ("that we may understand what God has freely given to us. . . . [T]hey are spiritually discerned," vv. 12, 14).[3] Human reason in its natural state is fallen, darkened by sin (Eph 4:17-18) and needs to be regenerated and renewed by the Holy Spirit (Col 3:10). There is a natural tendency of the fallen human mind to suppress the truth of God in unrighteousness (Rom 1:18), despite the fact that the existence of God and his power and divine nature are revealed in nature and the human conscience (Rom 1:19-20; 2:14-15).[4] When we become children of God by adoption, the Spirit supervenes directly upon our human spirits to give us a personal, experiential knowledge of God's love and fatherly character ("by him [the Spirit] we cry, '*Abba*, Father'" [Rom 8:15]; "God sent the Spirit of his Son into our hearts, the Spirit who calls out, '*Abba*, Father'" [Gal 4:6]).

We may note the presuppositions regarding *ontology* and *anthro-*

---

[3]On the long tradition of a doctrine of the *illumination* of divinely revealed words by the Holy Spirit in Christian theology, including but not limited to Augustine, Bonaventure, Aquinas and Calvin, see Benjamin B. Warfield, "Calvin's Doctrine of the Knowledge of God," and "Augustine's Doctrine of Knowledge and Authority," in *Calvin and Augustine* (Philadelphia: Presbyterian & Reformed, 1974), pp. 29-130, 387-477; Bonaventure, *The Mind's Journey into God*, in *The Essential Writings of Christian Mysticism*, ed. Bernard McGinn (New York: Modern Library, 2006), pp. 162-71; Lucien J. Richard, *The Spirituality of John Calvin* (Atlanta: John Knox Press, 1974), pp. 136-66; on Aquinas and the Thomistic tradition in epistemology see Jacques Maritain, "Knowledge by Connaturality," in *Distinguish to Unite: The Degrees of Knowledge* (London: Geoffrey Bles, 1959), pp. 260-62.

[4]On the general revelation of God in nature and conscience, see Bruce A. Demarest, *General Revelation: Historical Views and Contemporary Issues* (Grand Rapids: Zondervan, 1982); on the "noetic effects of sin," or the darkening of the human mind in matters moral and spiritual, see Stephen K. Moroney, *The Noetic Effects of Sin: A Historical and Contemporary Exploration of How Sin Affects Our Thinking* (Lanham, Md.: Lexington Books, 1999).

pology that stand behind Paul's logopneumatic epistemology. Paul knows that *words* and things *spiritual* in nature are not less real than visible, molecular objects. In fact, given the eternal existence of the triune God, Father, Son and Holy Spirit, and given the eternal and necessary existence of God's invisible spiritual essence, the *invisible* and the *spiritual* actual have ontological and logical primacy over the material and the visible. God has existed eternally and necessarily; visible matter has not existed eternally, but began to be when God spoke it into being; matter exists contingently, not necessarily.

Linguisticality—words, communication—is intrinsic to the eternal being of God (in the beginning was the *Logos* [Jn 1:1]); words as means of personal communion preexisted the creation of matter, being eternally present within the Trinity. Consequently, we can recognize that *materiality* is derivative from *linguisticality* and spirit—not the other way around. As in the biblical understanding of creation, the material world is *spoken* into being by the powerful, creative Word of God: Word and Spirit create matter—not vice versa.

As regards anthropology, it is a "normal" and not extraordinary state of affairs for humans to know spiritual things, for the human as the image of God, and who has a spirit (body, soul and *spirit* [1 Thess 5:23]), was created for the purpose of knowing God in personal relationship—God who is spirit (Jn 4:24).[5]

While this is a book on meditation, not a treatise on epistemology directed to academic philosophers, a few words are in order as to how this approach to the theory of knowledge relates to some generally recognized philosophical categories. This proposal for a logopneumatic epistemology can be understood, for example, in relation to the concept of *critical realism* and the doctrine of *analogy* in religious language. In the term *critical realism*, the word *realism* signifies the view that in our acts of valid knowing, our minds are actually making contact with a real world outside our minds.[6]

---

[5]On Paul's distinction of spirit from soul and body in man, see Robert Jewett, *Paul's Anthropological Terms* (Leiden: E. J. Brill, 1971). "Spirit" is that part of man that is sensitive to and open to the transcendent and to the Spirit of God.

[6]For an accessible and cogent defense of critical realism in epistemology, see John Searle, "Reality and Truth: The Default Position," "Four Challenges to Realism," "Skepticism, Knowledge,

Our acts of knowing, while they involve representations in our minds, do not merely terminate upon those representations, but our minds and bodies are in actual contact with an environment outside our minds and that exists independently of the mind. When I am looking at a tree, for example, the rays of light reflected from the tree that form an image on the retina of my eyes, which is then processed by my brain and categorized as a tree, actually bring my mind and its representations into a form of physical contact with the tree that exists outside my mind.

This realism is qualified by the term *critical* in order to acknowledge the fact that my knowledge of the tree, as mediated by the rays of light and images formed on my retinas, is selective, contextual, perspectival and analogical, not exhaustive. I have a valid experience and knowledge of the tree, but I do not know it exhaustively from a God's-eye point of view of an omniscient being. I cannot see the tree, for example, in ordinary observation, at the level of microscopic and atomic detail that could be provided by an electron microscope, but nevertheless, I have a genuine degree of knowledge of the tree.

The point of view in this book could be termed *critical spiritual realism*, to signify the view that God exists objectively outside the human mind and is not just an idea or representation created by the mind; that God is knowable, through Word, Spirit and the created order by the human mind and spirit; and that our knowledge of God and other spiritual realities is partial and analogical, not exhaustive.

As a realistic theory, critical spiritual realism asserts a real contact of the human spirit with the Holy Spirit ("He who unites himself with the Lord is one with him in spirit" [1 Cor 6:17; see 1 Cor 12:13], Spirit-to-spirit contact), and, through the mediation of the Holy Spirit, with divine things. To cite what could be called "Calvin's axiom," the Holy Spirit "truly unites [connects] things separated in space."[7] Just as the rays of light illuminate the tree and visually connect the tree to my retina, my brain and the representations of the tree in my brain and consciousness, so the Holy Spirit illuminates the things of creation

---

and Reality," and "Is There Any Justification for External Realism," in *Mind, Language and Society: Philosophy in the Real World* (New York: Basic Books, 1998), pp. 12-33.

[7]John Calvin, *Institutes of the Christian Religion* 4.17.10.

(Rom 1:20; general revelation) and the divinely revealed words of the Father given to the Son to share with us (Jn 14:25-26; 16:12-15; cf. 1 Cor 2:10-14; special revelation).

Critical spiritual realism rejects the dogmatic claim of Kant that God cannot be an object of religious experience.[8] God in fact has revealed himself to us and provided the basis for genuine knowledge of himself in creation, conscience and Scripture. The history of the human race shows that some awareness of an unseen spiritual reality that transcends our everyday interactions with molecules in the visible light range of the electromagnetic spectrum is present in all cultures. Some form of religious awareness seems to be, anthropologically speaking, a virtually universal phenomenon.

Critical spiritual realism is connected to a doctrine of the *analogical* nature of religious language and of our knowledge of God. It is held that our knowledge of God and our language of God is analogical, not equivocal or univocal (literal). A classic expression of this understanding of the analogical nature of religious language is found in Aquinas: "things are said of God and creatures analogically, and not in a purely equivocal nor in a purely univocal sense. . . . [I]n analogies the idea is not, as it is in univocals, one and the same, yet it is not totally diverse as in equivocals."[9]

For example, when God reveals himself as Father, this is not to say that God is exactly like a human father (univocal predication), nor is it to be understood that God in no way resembles a human father (equivocal predication), but rather that in significant respects God is like (analogous to) a human father—or, to be more biblically precise,

---

[8]For a critique of Kant's position on religious knowledge, see John Jefferson Davis, "Kant and the Problem of Religious Knowledge," in *Perspectives on Evangelical Theology*, ed. Kenneth S. Kantzer and Stanley N. Gundry (Grand Rapids: Baker, 1979), pp. 231-50; Alvin Plantinga, *Warranted Christian Belief* (New York: Oxford University Press, 2000), pp. 3-20, arguing that Kant has failed to demonstrate his claim that the categories of our minds cannot apply to God: "By way of conclusion, then, it doesn't look as if there is good reason in Kant or in the neighborhood of Kant for the conclusion that our concepts do not apply to God" (ibid., p. 30). For a sustained (and complex) argument for how religious experience can give epistemic warrant for belief in God, and for how religious experience is in some sense analogous to empirical experience, see William P. Alston, *Perceiving God: The Epistemology of Religious Experience* (Ithaca, N.Y.: Cornell University Press, 1991).

[9]Aquinas, *Summa Theologica*, 1, Q.13, art. 5 pt. 1.

human fathers are in some respects similar though not identical to the divine Father, who is the paradigm of all fatherhood (cf. Eph 3:14). God is certainly infinitely more than a human father, as to his power and perfections, but he is certainly not less. Similarly, when Scripture speaks of God's hand, this does not mean that God (strictly speaking, prior to the incarnation of the Son) has a physical body or literally has a hand, but rather that God as a personal being has the power to extend his will into our world and make things happen.

The doctrine of analogy in critical spiritual realism sees not only the divinely revealed words of Scripture as being the medium for our analogical knowledge of spiritual things, but the things of creation as well. This notion of the things of the molecular creation being fit to communicate to us analogical knowledge of the unseen things of God and the spiritual world is implied in what the apostle Paul writes in Romans 1:19-20:

> What *may be known* about God is plain to them [Gentiles], because God has made it plain to them. For since the creation of the world God's invisible qualities—his eternal power and divine nature—*have been clearly seen*, being understood from *what has been made*, so that men are without excuse. (emphasis added)

Paul is saying here that though God, as to his essence, is not a molecular entity manifesting in the visible light range, some of the divine attributes of God—for example, his power and wisdom—are in fact knowable through that which is molecular and visible. The visible, molecular things of this creation are the media of our partial and analogical yet valid knowledge of the invisible God. Water is a fitting image and analogy of the life-giving Spirit of God; bread is a fitting analogy for the words of God that are the true bread of heaven.

Scientists now recognize, in the so-called cosmic coincidences, that the laws of nature are remarkably fine-tuned so as to make the earth hospitable to life.[10] Just as the basic constants of nature—the strength of

---

[10]On the fine-tuning of the basic laws of physics, without which carbon-based life would not be possible, see Martin Rees, *Just Six Numbers: The Deep Forces that Shape the Universe* (New York: Basic Books, 2000); on the remarkable conditions in the solar system that make life on earth possible, see Peter D. Ward and Donald Brownlee, *Rare Earth: Why Complex Life Is Uncommon*

gravity, the electromagnetic force, the strong nuclear force within the atom and so on—are fine-tuned to make life possible, we can see, by extension, how the properties of the physical world are also fine-tuned to serve as the media for our analogical knowledge of unseen things.

When Paul says in Ephesians 1:4 that in God's eternal purpose, "he [the Father] chose us [the church] in him [Christ, the Son] before the creation of the world"—he is saying that God's purpose to create and redeem us preceded his actual creation of the material universe; the physical universe and laws of nature were designed to be consistent with and the means by which his saving purposes could be carried out. In other words, the laws of nature were decreed by God to be what they are in light of the divine purpose to create carbon-based human beings like us!

Just as it was not accidental that people, places and events in the Old Testament could be types, analogies and foreshadowings of things in the New Testament—but rather a consequence of the sovereign wisdom of God who determines all things according to his plan and will (Eph 1:11)—so it is not accidental that water, bread, fire, rocks and so forth can be analogies of spiritual things. They were created and designed with these purposes in mind; water was created to satisfy our thirst, to support life and also to serve as a fitting image of the Spirit of God.

This logopneumatic epistemology has some very practical implications for our practice of biblical meditation. The *logos* or word aspect of this biblical epistemology reminds us that reality is linguistic to the core, that words and the Word/Logos are an essential feature of the inner life of the triune God. Words are not human inventions but finite and analogical images of the communication that has always existed within the life of God as Father, Son and Holy Spirit. While there is certainly an important place and time for periods of silence and wordless contemplation and adoration in the presence of God (cf. "Be still, and know that I am God" [Ps 46:10]; "I have stilled and quieted my soul . . . like a weaned child is my soul within me" [Ps 131:2]), Christian meditation is not a "flight from the word" but embedded solidly in the context of the words of the biblical text.[11]

---

in the Universe (New York: Springer-Verlag, 2000).

[11]Unlike meditation in Zen Buddhism, which seeks enlightenment or *satori* by emptying the

The *pneumatic* aspect of this biblical realized epistemology reminds us that our personal, experiential knowledge of God always involves both word *and* Spirit. It is the Spirit of God who reveals the things of Christ to us and illuminates them to our hearts and minds, and puts us into actual contact with the spiritual realities signified in the biblical texts. Words alone without Spirit can *dry us up;* Spirit alone without the words of Scripture (and the fellowship of the church), can *blow us up;* but with Word and Spirit in proper balance, we can *grow up* in our knowledge and experience of the loving presence of God. Consequently, the Spirit is always of vital importance as we come to the Scriptures to meditate. As we place ourselves in the presence of God and pray for God to send the Spirit upon the Word, they can become for us words of spirit and life (Jn 6:63), and the means of joyful communion with the risen One with whom we live in communion, as living branches in the living Vine.

BIBLIOLOGY
THE ONTOLOGY AND TELEOLOGY OF SCRIPTURE

Bibliology is the technical term in theology for the doctrine of Scripture. A fully developed doctrine of Scripture would include answers to such questions as: What *is* the Bible (ontology)? What reality or realities does it represent? And what are the purposes (teleology) for which the Bible was given to the people of God? This discussion will suggest some answers to these questions, which are related to the earlier discussions of the Trinity, union with Christ and inaugurated eschatology.

It may seem odd to even raise the question of what the Bible is, for in an evangelical context the answer is obvious: the Bible is a sacred text whose words are inspired by the Holy Spirit. Such an understanding is supported by classic texts in the New Testament such as 2 Timothy 3:16-17: "All Scripture (*pasa graphē*) is God-breathed (*theopneustos*) and useful for teaching, rebuking, correcting and training in righteousness, so that the man of God may be thoroughly equipped for every good

---

mind of words and conceptual distinctions. See Shunryu Suzuki, *Zen Mind, Beginner's Mind: Informal Talks on Zen Meditation and Practice* (New York: Weatherill, 1970); D. T. Suzuki, *An Introduction to Zen Buddhism* (New York: Grove Press, 1964).

work."[12] It is sometimes valuable to step back from the obvious and to take a fresh look at a familiar object (or person) and to ask ourselves if there are other aspects that we have missed or forgotten.

In the case of the Bible, I want to suggest that the obvious answer— "the Bible is a written document inspired by God"—is a correct and fundamental one, but one that for the purposes of biblical meditation needs to be enhanced and enriched by the recognition of other aspects of God's revelation to us. Specifically, I want to highlight three additional dimensions of our understanding of biblical revelation: the Bible as *living* Word, the Bible as *ecclesial* Word, and the Bible as a *cultural-linguistic world*.

The writer of the epistle to the Hebrews tells us that "the word of God is living and active. Sharper than any double-edged sword" (Heb 4:12). This characterization of the word of God as *living* reminds us that Scripture as written *text*—the form in which modern Christians most often encounter Scripture—is nevertheless intimately connected with three nonwritten realities, namely, Jesus Christ, the living Word; the Holy Spirit; and oral discourse. The Scriptures are not only inspired by the Holy Spirit at their points of origin (1 Cor 2:13) but also *illuminated* by the Holy Spirit at their points of personal reception (1 Cor 2:12, 14).

The words of Christ are spirit and life (Jn 6:63); they are, by the Spirit's illuminating presence, the living words of the living Christ speaking to us in the actuality of the present moment. The words of Scripture, when illuminated by the Spirit, impart the life of God to our souls and strengthen faith. Calvin could even say that "without the illumination of the Holy Spirit, the Word can do nothing," but with the Spirit, the believer can "taste the truth of God" and "his heart is established therein."[13] Just as within the life of the Trinity, the second person is distinct from but not separated from the third person, so in the life of the church and Christian devotion, the objective truth of the Word (biblical text as

---

[12]For a classic discussion of this text and of the doctrine of the inspiration of the Scriptures generally, see Benjamin B. Warfield, *The Inspiration and Authority of the Bible* (Philadelphia: Presbyterian & Reformed, 1948); see also Carl F. H. Henry, "The Meaning of Inspiration," in *God, Revelation, and the Bible* (Waco, Tex.: Word, 1979), 4:129-61.

[13]Calvin, *Institutes* 3.2.33, "The Word becomes efficacious for our faith through the Holy Spirit."

given) is distinct from but not separate from the illuminating personal presence of the Spirit (biblical text as illuminated) in the heart.

The historic theologies of the Reformation have affirmed both the objective inspiration of the Scriptures in history and their subjective illumination in Christian experience, but in the modern period, in reaction to critical attacks on the authority of Scripture, most conservative attention has been focused on the objective side (that is, inspiration). The articulation of the illuminating work of the Spirit has understandably focused primarily, though not exclusively, on the noetic or cognitive dimensions (for example, attestation to the divine truth of the biblical text).

In the classic statement found in the Westminster Confession of Faith (1646) it is stated that with respect to the inspired Scriptures, "our full persuasion and assurance of the infallible truth, and divine authority thereof, is from the inward work of the Holy Spirit, bearing witness by and with the Word in our hearts."[14] In the context of the post-Reformation Catholic-Protestant debates over the authority of Scripture and the church, the Westminster divines emphasized the "self-authenticating" nature of biblical authority and the witness of the Holy Spirit.

A modern statement on illumination by the evangelical theologians Gordon Lewis and Bruce Demarest also highlights the cognitive aspects of the Spirit's work in this regard: "illumination enables sinners to understand that the gospel is objectively true, to assent to its truth for themselves personally, and to commit themselves to the Savior."[15] Divine illumination, they note, "produces no new revelation" but "opens the mind and will to the reception of revelation (1 Cor 2:14)."[16]

The illuminating work of the Spirit in informing the mind as to truth and engaging the will for trust and obedience is well attested in the Scripture. Here, however, in the context of a discussion of meditating on Scripture, I would like also to draw attention to the *affective* dimensions of the Spirit's illuminating work. The Holy Spirit, who pours the love of God into our hearts (Rom 5:5) and who replicates

---

[14]Westminster Confession of Faith, chap. 1, par. 5.
[15]Gordon R. Lewis and Bruce A. Demarest, *Integrative Theology* (Grand Rapids: Zondervan, 1987), 1:167.
[16]Ibid., p. 116.

the prayer language of Jesus to his Father in our hearts (*"Abba*, Father" [Rom 8:15; Gal 4:6]), draws us into the loving and joyful communion of Father, Son and Holy Spirit. Jesus' words are spoken to the disciples so that they "may have the full measure of my joy within them" (Jn 17:13), and the Holy Spirit enables us to enter into this joy as we sense the presence of God ("you will fill me with joy in your presence" [Ps 16:11]) through faithful meditation on the Word and by virtue of our union with Christ in the Spirit. God is present to us through the biblical Word as the living Christ speaks to us by his Spirit. The presence of the Holy Spirit in and through the text not only illuminates truth in some objective, propositional sense (though it is indeed this) but is *God himself* present to us through the text and by faith; the Holy Spirit is God himself present to us and speaking to us, communicating to us the Father's love for the Son and the Son's joy in being loved by the Father.

The Scriptures were inspired and preserved as written texts so that we might enjoy communion and fellowship with the living God who loves us. The apostle John stated that he was writing his epistle so that "you may also have fellowship with us," who have been drawn into the communion of "the Father and with his Son, Jesus" (1 Jn 1:3). The inspiration of the Scriptures in history and the illumination of the Scriptures in Christian experience need then always to be held together in balance, and the affective dimensions of illumination affirmed together with the cognitive and volitional. As we meditate on the Scriptures we do so in the hope that our minds will be informed, our wills strengthened to obey and our affections warmed by the love and joy of God.

The characterization of the Scriptures as living words (Jn 6:63; Heb 4:12) not only points to their dynamic, life-giving nature, but also reminds us of the aspect of orality as well.[17] It is easy to forget that in many cases the people of God encountered God's words in

---

[17]On the significance of orality in the history of communication and cultures, see Walter J. Ong, *Orality and Literacy: The Technologizing of the Word* (London: Methuen, 1962); and his *The Presence of the Word: Some Prolegomena for Cultural and Religious History* (Minneapolis: University of Minnesota Press, 1981).

spoken form before these words were made available in writing. Moses reminded the people that they heard the living voice of God speaking from Mount Sinai (Deut 4:10-12) before those words of the covenant were recorded on the tablets of stone and deposited in the ark of the covenant in the tabernacle. The spoken word is found in the context of one person being present to another; God's spoken word was in the contexts of his presence to his people in the midst of the gathered assembly.

This emphasis on *hearing* the Word of God (as distinguished from reading it) is enshrined in the most important prayer of the old covenant, the *Shema:* "Hear, O Israel: The LORD our God, the LORD is one" (Deut 6:4). Day after day Ezra the scribe read the book of the law of Moses to the returning exiles assembled before the Water Gate in Jerusalem (Neh 8).

Jesus reads from the scroll of Isaiah in the Nazareth synagogue, proclaiming its fulfillment in himself, the Spirit-anointed Servant of the Lord (Lk 4:16-21). Paul reminded the Thessalonians that before they had his gospel in written form, it had been preached to them orally, "not simply with words, but also with power, with the Holy Spirit and with deep conviction" (1 Thess 1:5). Before the epistle we know as 1 Peter was written, Peter reminds his readers that the gospel had been *preached* to them by the Holy Spirit sent from heaven (1 Pet 1:12) and that they had been spiritually reborn "through the living and enduring word of God" (1 Pet 1:23). Paul instructs Timothy to make the public reading of Scripture—reading and hearing of the Word—a priority of his ministry in Ephesus (1 Tim 4:13).

The significance for the practice of meditation of this *oral* dimension of divine revelation is that it reminds us of the importance of *listening*, *attentiveness* and *receptivity* as we approach the Scriptures. When we approach a written text, we can have the sense of being in control of the text and using it for our own purposes. As the *Shema* (Deut 6:4) reminds us, our first obligation is to place ourselves in the presence of God and his Word in an attentive, receptive and noncontrolling stance, and to wait to hear God's voice. "*Today*, if you *hear* his voice, do not harden your hearts" (Heb 4:7; Ps 95:7-8, emphasis added). The writer of Hebrews, who knows that the words of God are living (Heb 4:12), here witnesses to the fact that the ancient inspired texts of Scripture (for example, Ps 95:7-8) come alive and speak with God's living, contemporary voice as they are illuminated by the Spirit: God the Father actually speaks to us through the living Son by the Spirit—"today" (Heb 4:7).

The Scriptures are not only living words but also *ecclesial* words. The natural home of the Bible is not the university or the classroom, but the church and the community of faith. When God spoke to the people from Mount Sinai, the words of the living God were in the midst of the covenant assembly; the Ten Commandments and subsequent covenant documents were then deposited in the ark of the covenant in the taber-nacle, in the midst of the people, signifying the central place of the words of God for the life of the chosen people.

For the first fifteen hundred years or so of the history of the Christian church, prior to the invention of the printing press, the only access to the Scriptures that most Christians would have had would have been hearing them publicly read in the church during the liturgy. In the monastic setting, the chanting of the psalms and the reading of the Scriptures in the lectionary cycle was a communal event in the context of a faith community. It was only during the Enlightenment period and the growing dominance of the European research universities that the academic study of the Bible became separated from its earlier ecclesial and monastic settings.[18] In our time, we can recognize that a devotional and meditative reading of Scripture is not a second-class reading when compared with academic study, but in fact, very much in keeping with the primary purpose of Scripture—a document given by God to the people of God to nourish faith and piety.

Not only is the Bible a living word and an ecclesial word, it can also be seen as a cultural-linguistic *world*. That is to say, the Bible not only conveys information but also through its narratives, proverbs, poetry, epistles and varied literary forms, informs the Christian *imagination* and

---

[18]For a survey of the history of the rise of the modern critical study of the Bible in university settings, see Alexa Suelzer, "Modern Old Testament Criticism," in *The Jerome Biblical Com-mentary*, ed. Raymond E. Brown, Joseph Fitzmyer and Roland E. Murphy (Englewood Cliffs, N.J.: Prentice-Hall, 1968), pp. 590-604.

paints a picture of an alternative universe, as it were—the world to come—which is a dwelling place for the Christian heart and imagination. George Lindbeck has argued that all religions, with their doctrines, rituals and symbols, constitute a kind of "cultural and/or linguistic framework that shapes the entirety of life and thought."[19] "Like a culture or language," such a cultural-linguistic world, according to Lindbeck, "is a communal phenomenon that shapes the subjectivities of individuals rather than being primarily a manifestation of those subjectivities."[20]

The modern world and the scientific revolution have drained the Christian imagination of much of its ability to live out of a compelling vision of a coming world that transcends the present one.[21] Saturating the Christian heart and mind with the doctrines and images and stories of Scripture in the practices of prayer and meditation can build a Christian counterculture of the mind (cf. Rom 12:1-2) that can help the Christian to resist and push back against the secularizing forces of modernity and postmodernity, and strengthen our ability to keep our minds and imaginations focused on the heavenly realities above (Col 3:1-2).

On the teleology of Scripture. I would like to conclude this section with a few observations on the teleology of Scripture in relation to the practice of biblical meditation. The question here is, For what purposes did God give the Bible to the church? The form in which the question has been posed deliberately suggests that we need to recognize multiple purposes and functions of Scripture in the life of faith, not merely one.

We can recognize at least four functions or purposes of Scripture in the community of faith: the *informative*, the *transformative*, the *imaginative* and the *unitive*. The first two are widely recognized and are not problematic; the latter two are not self-evident and require a bit of justification.

---

[19]George Lindbeck, *The Nature of Doctrine: Religion and Theology in a Postliberal Age* (Philadelphia: Westminster Press, 1984), p. 33. In relation to Lindbeck, I want to stress the fact that from an orthodox and evangelical perspective, such a cultural-linguistic world is not only descriptive of the subjective beliefs and symbols of a particular religious community, but actually makes truth claims that are rooted in history and realities external to the community.

[20]Ibid.

[21]On the displacement of the biblical narrative as a compelling imaginative vision by the scientific revolution, see Hans Frei, *The Eclipse of the Biblical Narrative: A Study in Eighteenth and Nineteenth Century Hermeneutics* (New Haven, Conn.: Yale University Press, 1974).

A classic text on the inspiration of the Bible such as 2 Timothy 3:16 ("All Scripture is God-breathed and is useful for teaching, rebuking, correcting and training in righteousness") clearly points to the informative (teaching) and transformative (rebuking, correcting, training) dimensions. As we study, teach and preach the Scriptures, our purpose is to inform ourselves and others with sound doctrine and to shape Christian behavior and character.

I would argue that believing meditation on the Scriptures, when illuminated by the Holy Spirit, can function in all four dimensions: informative, transformative, imaginative and unitive. By imaginative I mean the function of Scripture in opening up our minds to the reality of the unseen, heavenly age to come that is already arriving—a countercultural biblical consciousness (Rom 12:1-2) that gives us the cognitive resources to push back against the accommodating forces of worldliness. By unitive I mean the function of Scripture, by virtue of our union with Christ and the illuminating action of the Holy Spirit, to bring us into an awareness and actual experience of the enjoyable presence of Christ (cf. "I say these things . . . so that they may have the full measure of my joy within them" [Jn 17:13]).

Especially for those of us who may be seminarians, pastors or other religious professionals, it is good to be reminded of the fact that Scripture was given not only for the purpose of providing information and instruction for ourselves and others—sermon outlines and Bible studies—but also, and more finally, for bringing us into the enjoyment of communion with the Lord who loves us, and who is really present to us through the Scriptures.

6

THE HERMENEUTICS OF
THE AGE TO COME

Inaugurated Eschatology and Recovering
the Ancient Fourfold Sense of Scripture

∿∿
∿∿

In the previous section I argued that inaugurated eschatology—the new "already" of the new creation ushered in by the resurrection of Jesus Christ, his exaltation to the Father's right hand and the
outpouring of the Holy Spirit—was the basis for a radically new biblical
ontology and worldview. In this section I will argue that inaugurated eschatology also implies a new way of reading and meditating on Scripture.
More specifically, I argue for a recovery of the fourfold sense of Scripture
in the ancient church as a legitimate way of faithfully meditating on the
Scriptures, on the basis of the presence of the Holy Spirit in the church
and our union with Christ in his heavenly, exalted state.

From the time of John Cassian (d. 435) in the early church it was
common to distinguish senses of Scripture other than and in addition to
the literal or historical-grammatical sense.[1] The tropological or moral
sense related to behavior or ethics (cf. Deut 25:4, "do not muzzle an ox
while it is treading out the grain," referred to by Paul to the wages of a
church leader [1 Tim 5:17-18]). The allegorical sense referred to the fore-
shadowing of Christ or the church in the types of the Old Testament (for

---

[1] James Samuel Preus, *From Shadow to Promise: Old Testament Interpretation from Augustine to the Young Luther* (Cambridge, Mass.: Harvard University Press, 1969), pp. 21-23, 26-37; see espe-cially the magisterial study of Henri de Lubac, *The Four Senses of Scripture*, vol. 1 of *Medieval Exegesis*, trans. Mark Sebanc (Grand Rapids: Eerdmans, 1998).

example, the serpent lifted up in the wilderness as a type of the cross of Christ [Jn 3:14]). The anagogical or heavenly sense is found in the events and institutions of the old covenant foreshadowings of the eternal, heavenly state (for example, "the Jerusalem that is above . . . is our mother" [Gal 4:26]; cf. Heb 12:18-22: the earthly and heavenly Mount Zions).

I speak here of a retrieval of the ancient fourfold sense of Scripture against the background of two powerful influences in church history: the Protestant Reformers' reactions against medieval allegorizing and their renewed emphasis on the historical-grammatical sense, and the rise of the Enlightenment's historical-critical method that essentially limited valid biblical meaning to the historical sense alone. The Reformers of the sixteenth century, benefiting from Erasmus's critical edition of the Greek New Testament, Renaissance humanism's new interest in primary historical source documents, and the revived studies of the Hebrew language, understandably reacted against the allegorizing methods of the ancient and medieval church, which, in their estimation, had obscured the true meaning of Scripture and the clarity of the gospel itself.[2]

The rise of the historical-critical method during the Enlightenment and the academic study of the Bible in the modern European university settings devalued the patristic and medieval interpretive traditions, and saw the literal or historical meaning of the text as essentially the *only* valid meaning. A classic statement of this modern critical view of biblical interpretation is found in the famous 1859 essay of Benjamin Jowett, then Regius Professor of Greek at Oxford University, "On the Interpretation of Scripture."[3] Professor Jowett announced that "it may be laid down that Scripture has one meaning—the meaning which it had to the mind of the prophet or evangelist who first uttered or wrote, to the hearers or readers who first received it."[4] *Interpret the Scripture like any other book.* "Scripture, like other books, has one meaning, which is to be gathered from itself without reference to the adaptations of Fathers or Divines; and without regard to *a priori* notions about its nature and

---

[2]On the new currents in Renaissance and Reformation interpretation of Scripture, see William Yarchin, *History of Biblical Interpretation* (Peabody, Mass.: Hendrickson, 2004), pp. 171-94.

[3]Benjamin Jowett, "On the Interpretation of Scripture," in *Essays and Reviews* (1860; reprint, London: John W. Parker, 1970).

[4]Ibid., p. 378.

origins."[5] An implication, for example, of Jowett's views, which since have become orthodoxy in the academic study of the Bible, is that in a text such as Isaiah 7:14, whatever the church fathers (or Matthew [Mt 7:22]) might have thought, the historical Isaiah surely could not have intended to predict the virgin birth of God's Messiah, as fulfilled in Jesus; Isaiah was speaking only to his own time and circumstances.

I believe that Jowett is deeply mistaken and his position needs to be questioned on the basis of the following six considerations: (1) his theological presuppositions and view of biblical inspiration, (2) the interpretation of the Old Testament by Christ and the apostles, (3) the renewed recognition in biblical scholarship of the proper role of biblical typology, (4) fresh insights from modern patristic scholarship on biblical interpretation in the ancient church, (5) recognition of some common misunderstandings of patristic and medieval exegesis, and most significantly (6) the reality of inaugurated eschatology, the presence of the Spirit and the believer's union with Christ. My purpose is not to deny the primacy of the historical-grammatical meaning but to argue for the validity, in certain cases, of the christological and heavenly senses.[6]

Jowett's essay was published in a collection of essays, *Essays and Reviews* (1860), whose authors represented liberalizing tendencies in the Church of England at the time.[7] Jowett made no secret of his lack of enthusiasm for the historic doctrine of the verbal inspiration of the Bible:

> If the term inspiration were to fall into disuse, no fact of nature, or history . . . no event in the life of man, or dealings of God with him, would be in any degree altered. . . . [T]he interpreter . . . had better go on his way and leave the more precise definition of the word to the progress of knowledge and the results of the study of Scripture, instead of entangling himself with a theory about it.[8]

---

[5]Ibid., pp. 377, 404.

[6]I am using the term *christological* sense as a synonym for the allegorical sense, which can refer to Christ and the church, but I wish to avoid the term *allegorical* because of the negative associations of this term in the modern period.

[7]"As a protest against the minimizing spirit of the volume, 11,000 of the [Church of England] clergy declared their belief in the inspiration of the Scriptures . . . and the book was at length synodically condemned in 1864" ("Essays and Reviews," *Oxford Dictionary of the Christian Church*, ed. F. L. Cross [London: Oxford University Press, 1958], p. 463).

[8]Jowett, "On the Interpretation of Scripture," p. 351.

In distancing himself from the historic Christian view that the Holy
Spirit had actually superintended and inspired the words of the human
authors of the Scriptures, Jowett was also leaving behind the historic
view that all the Scriptures formed a coherent whole, with events,
persons and institutions of the old covenant divinely and providentially
ordained to point to their greater fulfillment in the new. This "single
meaning" theory of interpretation was premised on a view of inspiration
fundamentally out of accord with the view of Christ and the apostles
and the historic, orthodox traditions of the church, both East and West.[9]

The restriction of the meaning of a biblical text to *only* a historical-
grammatical sense as understood by the original author is inconsistent
with the way that Christ and the apostles interpreted the Old Testament.[10]
Christ taught that the Hebrew Scriptures, as a whole, testified to himself
(Jn 5:39); Moses wrote about him (Jn 5:46); his sufferings, death and resurrection were foretold in the law of Moses, the Prophets and the Psalms
(Lk 24:44). The crossing of the Red Sea was a type of Christian baptism
(1 Cor 10:2); the water from the rock and the manna in the wilderness
were types or foreshadowings of the Lord's Supper (1 Cor 10:3-4); the
bronze serpent lifted up in the wilderness by Moses was a type of the cross
(Jn 3:14); Hagar and Sarah were figures of the old and new covenants (Gal
4:24); the earthly tabernacle was a type and shadow of the heavenly one
(Heb 9:23-24); the flood was a type of Christian baptism (1 Pet 3:21) and
so forth. These examples are well known and could be multiplied.[11] They
do not fit easily (or at all) with Jowett's restrictive single-meaning theory,

---

[9]See John Wenham, *Christ and the Bible* (Grand Rapids: Baker, 1984); Benjamin B. Warfield,
The Inspiration and Authority of the Bible (Philadelphia: Presbyterian & Reformed, 1948); on
the history of the doctrine of inspiration in the patristic and medieval periods, see Cristiano
Pesch, *De Inspiratione Sacra Scripturae* (Freiburg: Herder, 1906).

[10]See Walter C. Kaiser, "The Typological Use of the Old Testament in the New," in *The Uses of
the Old Testament in the New* (Chicago: Moody Press, 1985), pp. 103-41; G. K. Beale, ed., *The
Right Doctrine from the Wrong Texts?* (Grand Rapids: Baker, 1994), pp. 331-71.

[11]The evangelical New Testament scholar Richard Longenecker expressed ambivalence toward
such phenomena in his article "Can We Reproduce the Exegesis of the New Testament?"
Tyndale Bulletin 21 (1970): 3-38. "Our commitment as Christians is to the reproduction of the
apostolic faith and doctrine, and only secondarily (if at all) to the specific apostolic exegetical
practices" (ibid., p. 38). Longenecker's ambivalence notwithstanding, it remains indisputably
the case that Christ and the apostles did find typological levels of meaning in the Old Testament texts. The volume edited by Beale, *The Right Doctrine from the Wrong Texts?* is a comprehensive response to some of Longenecker's concerns.

but in such cases, the historic, orthodox hermeneutical tradition of the church East and West has sided not with Jowett and critical scholars, but with Christ and the apostles.

In a healthy reaction to the atomistic tendencies of critical biblical scholarship in much of the eighteenth and nineteenth centuries, more recent biblical scholarship has attempted to recover a sense of the canonical shape of Scripture and has argued for renewed recognition of the typological use of the Old Testament by the New Testament writers, in the context of redemptive history. Notable in this regard was the seminal work of the German New Testament scholar Leonhard Goppelt, *Typos: The Typological Interpretation of the Old Testament in the New,* based on his 1939 dissertation, and the 1957 work of G. W. H. Lampe and K. J. Woollcombe, *Essays on Typology.*[12]

Among evangelical scholars the Tyndale House Old Testament Lecture for 1955 by Francis Foulkes, "The Acts of God: A Study of the Basis of Typology in the Old Testament," was a groundbreaking work in this recovery.[13] Conservative scholars had never abandoned the historic recognition of typology, but these contributions of Goppelt, Lampe, Woollcombe and others were a recognition of the overly restrictive nature of a single-meaning theory to account for the realities of the biblical texts and their New Testament interpreters.[14]

---

[12]Leonhard Goppelt, *Typos: The Typological Interpretation of the Old Testament in the New* (Grand Rapids: Eerdmans, 1981); G. W. H. Lampe and K. J. Woollcombe, *Essays on Typology* (Naperville, Ill.: A. R. Allenson, 1957).

[13]Francis Foulkes, "The Acts of God: A Study of the Basis of Typology in the Old Testament," www.biblicalstudies.org.uk/pdf/tp/acts_of_god_foulkes.pdf. Foulkes made a convincing case for a proper distinction between allegory and typology, the latter being firmly rooted in the providentially ordained events of Old Testament history: "we find in the Old Testament the twofold basis of typology. We find that the belief in the unchanging God who is Lord of history leads to the understanding of the repetition of the acts of God. We find also that the Old Testament itself points forward to divine acts more glorious than any in the past. . . . There is to be a new David, but a greater David; a new Moses but a greater Moses. . . . There is to be a greater and more wonderful tabernacling of God, as His presence comes to dwell in a new temple" (ibid., pp. 32-33).

[14]For a helpful survey of both critical and conservative scholarship on the matter of typology, see G. P. Hugenberger, "Introductory Notes on Typology," in *The Right Doctrine from the Wrong Texts?* ed. G. K. Beale (Grand Rapids: Baker, 1994), pp. 331-33, noting the work of Walter Eichrodt, Gerhard von Rad, H. W. Wolff, Michael Fishbane, and others, and pp. 333-36, citing the work of Ernst Hengstenberg, Patrick Fairbairn, Milton Terry, Geerhardus Vos, Meredith G. Kline, Bernard Ramm, David Baker, S. Lewis Johnson, Moises Silva, Edmund Clowney, Vern Poythress and others. On the history of typological interpretation in Jonathan Edwards and the Puritans, see Mason Ira Lowance Jr., *Images and Shadows of Divine Things:*

Recent patristic scholarship has attempted to take more seriously the exegetical practices of the church fathers, letting them speak in their own voices rather than first filtering them through the polemical grids of the Catholic-Protestant debates of the Reformation period, or through the dismissive attitudes of nineteenth-century liberal Protestant scholars.[15] Recent patristic scholarship has helped to clarify the important distinction between an allegorizing approach to Scripture, rooted in a Neo-Platonic metaphysics, and a more Christian spiritual reading that is theologically grounded in redemptive history. When, for example, the fathers connected the person of Joshua with Jesus or the exodus with Christian baptism, they did so, according to O'Keefe and Reno, "not because they were tragically unschooled in historical method but because they saw these persons and events as in fact connected in the divine economy."[16]

In other words, the church fathers brought to the text a belief in the inspiration of the Scriptures and a conviction in the providential ordering of the history of Israel, and were able to connect the dots between the Old and New Testaments in appropriate ways.[17] Donald Fairbairn, in an insightful review article on patristic exegesis, has pointed out that modern theories of biblical interpretation like that of Jowett's reflect Enlight-

---

Puritan Typology in New England from 1660-1750 (Atlanta: microform, 1967).

[15]Notable in this regard is Rowan A. Greer, *The Captain of Our Salvation: A Study of the Patristic Exegesis of Hebrews* (Tubingen: Mohr, 1973); and John J. O'Keefe and R. R. Reno, *Sanctified Vision: An Introduction to Early Christian Interpretation of the Bible* (Baltimore: Johns Hopkins University Press, 2005); see also Manlio Simonetti, *Biblical Interpretation in the Early Church: An Historical Introduction to Patristic Exegesis* (Edinburgh: T & T Clark, 1994). The twenty-eight-volume *Ancient Christian Commentary on Scripture*, edited by Thomas C. Oden, spanning the seven-century period of patristic commentary from Clement of Alexandria to John of Damascus, is yet another notable sign of the renewed interest in the contributions of the church fathers to biblical interpretation.

[16]O'Keefe and Reno, *Sanctified Vision*, p. 87. They note that the patristic conviction that there is a "Christ-centered structure that organizes all biblical revelation has been replaced by the post-Enlightenment dogma that revelation is embedded in the events of history shaped by sociological, psychological, and cultural . . . forces. . . . The fathers had a faith in a divine economy in which . . . Jesus Christ's life, death, and resurrection is strangely more real, more interpretively powerful, than our own this-worldly experiences" (ibid., p. 88). This latter comment on the fathers is congruent with what I had earlier called the *imaginative* function of Scripture in providing an alternative *cultural world* through which this world was to be viewed.

[17]This is not to deny the fact that the fathers did at times indulge in allegorizing and fanciful exegesis; the point here is simply to recognize that their typological and spiritual readings could be seen as continuous with the readings of Christ and the apostles, and with the doctrines of inspiration and providence.

enment assumptions that "Scripture has to be assessed and judged, that it is not trustworthy, that we must dig deeply to get to the history behind the text."[18] "Why then," he asks evangelical scholars, "do we reject out of hand the patristic style of exegesis that shares our assumptions, in favor of a modern method of exegesis that utterly rejects our [Christian, biblical] worldview?"[19] The question is a good one, and deserves to be pondered.

Modern dismissive attitudes toward the fathers' finding of spiritual senses in the text are at times based on a serious misunderstanding, that is, the assumption that premodern exegesis did not recognize a primacy of the literal sense. Quite significantly, for example, Thomas Aquinas clearly affirms the priority of the literal sense: "the spiritual sense . . . is based on the literal, and presupposes it. . . . All the senses are founded on one—the literal—from which alone can any argument be drawn, and not from those intended in allegory, as Augustine says (*Epist.* 48)."[20] As if this were not clear enough, Aquinas goes on to say that "nothing necessary to faith is contained under the spiritual sense which is not elsewhere put forward by the Scripture in its literal sense."[21] Aquinas affirms the validity of spiritual senses found in the New Testament and patristic tradition, but articulates the normative place of the literal sense in a way that should satisfy the concerns of evangelical Protestant interpreters to guard against arbitrary and fanciful misuses of the biblical texts.[22]

Finally, and perhaps most importantly, I wish to argue that the retrieval of the ancient fourfold sense of Scripture is warranted by the two biblical-theological truths that have been central in this book: the realities of *union with Christ* and *inaugurated eschatology*. My concern is primarily with the christological and heavenly senses, since these are the two senses

---

[18]Donald Fairbairn, "Patristic Exegesis and Theology: The Cart and the Horse," *Westminster Theological Journal* 69 (2007): 18.

[19]Ibid. Related questions had been raised in 1980 by David C. Steinmetz in his widely read article "The Superiority of Pre-Critical Exegesis," *Theology Today* 37, no. 1 (1980): 27-38.

[20]Aquinas, "Whether in Holy Scripture a Word May Have Several Senses?" *Summa Theologica* 1.Q.1, art. 10.

[21]Ibid.

[22]The priority and foundational place of the literal sense was also strongly affirmed by the fourteenth-century scholar Nicholas of Lyra at the University of Paris. See Yarchin, "Medieval Recognition of the Literal Sense: Nicholas Lyra and the *Glossa ordinaria* on Psalm 23," in *History of Biblical Interpretation*, pp. 97-108; see also Philip D. W. Krey and Leslie Smith, eds., *Nicholas of Lyra: The Senses of Scripture*, Studies in the History of Christian Thought (Leiden: Brill, 2000).

of Scripture, especially the latter, that would seem to be most out of favor with modern exegetes. I want to show, with the aid of several specific examples, how the "two realities"—union with Christ and the presence of the Spirit and heavenly realities in inaugurated eschatology—can inform our recognition, in certain texts, of the christological and heavenly senses. And I also wish to argue that the now traditional Enlightenment reading of Scripture is saddled with three faulty assumptions.

I identify as faulty assumptions the following: (1) that Christ, from the time of his ascension to heaven, has been *absent* from the church and the believer's immediate experience, (2) that the believer's experience of heaven is exclusively *future*, and (3) that the history of redemption foreshadowed in the old covenant terminated with the cross and the empty tomb—rather than continuing with Christ's exaltation to heaven and his present reign at the right hand of the Father.

As to the first assumption, the New Testament makes it clear that Christ is not absent from the church or the believer. Christ is in fact present to the believer and to the church in a *threefold* way, despite the fact that Christ's glorified, molecular body is not present on earth but is now invisible in heaven.[23] Christ is really within the believer by the Holy Spirit, who extends Christ's self and presence into the believer's heart ("Christ in you, the hope of glory" [Col 1:27]); Christ is really *among* the believing assembly gathered as a church in worship, by virtue of his name and Spirit (1 Cor 5:4; the name and Spirit as extensions of Christ's self); and the believer is really present to the heavenly, ascended Christ, being seated with Christ in heavenly realms (Eph 2:6)—the Spirit connecting the believer with Christ and extending the believer's spirit and self to Christ's self (1 Cor 6:17). The Holy Spirit connects us with Christ and lifts us into the presence of the ascended Lord, with whom we are in union from the time of our conversion, being incorporated into the body of Christ by the Holy Spirit (1 Cor 12:13), who continues to abide in us as an ontological reality.

---

[23]The question where is Christ now? after the ascension and Pentecost needs an answer in terms of a threefold location of Christ, not merely a single location: Christ as to his molecular body is located in heaven, but Christ's extended self, as extended by means of his name (1 Cor 5:4; his Skype icon) and Spirit, is also simultaneously and really located in the midst of the worshiping assembly, and also within the heart of the believer: "Christ *above* us, in heaven; Christ *among* us, in worship; Christ *within* us in the heart, by his Spirit and promise."

The ascension does not mean the absence of Christ so much as it means the presence of Christ in *a new way*. He continues to be present in the midst of his believing disciples (Mt 18:20; 28:20; 1 Cor 5:4; Rev 3:20). Though his molecular body is now absent from and hidden from us, it was to *our advantage* that Christ ascended (Jn 16:7), because now that Jesus has sent the Holy Spirit to remain with us, Christ is actually present to believers in a more powerfully transformative and interior way than he was to the apostles during the evening of the Last Supper. When Christ returns at the end of history to inaugurate the new creation, he will be present to us in yet a more powerful way, with a glorified and transformed molecular body, surrounded by the fullness of the presence of the Holy Spirit, the Shekinah glory of God. We ourselves will experience his presence more intensely than now, with our own bodies and perceptual abilities being transformed and enhanced, and with a yet fuller and deeper interior experience of the Spirit.

The second faulty assumption is that the believer's experience of heaven is exclusively future: "going to heaven when we die." It is true, of course, that we will not fully enjoy the blessings of heaven and the new creation until the time when Christ returns to restore all things (cf. Acts 3:21). The reality of inaugurated eschatology, however, is that with the exaltation of Jesus and the arrival of the promised Holy Spirit, we already are beginning to experience the realities of heaven. The worshiping church is already tasting the goodness of the Word of God and the powers of the age to come (Heb 6:5). Because of the powerful efficacy of the atoning blood and finished work of Christ, we can now have confidence to enter into the heavenly holy of holies and draw near to God in full assurance of faith (Heb 10:19, 22). The believing, worshiping church is already in the presence of God, the heavenly Jerusalem and the joyful assembly of the angels and saints (Heb 12:22-24). We are already seated with Christ in heaven (Eph 2:6); the Holy Spirit unites us to Christ and lifts our spirits into the presence of his glorified, heavenly self.

The third faulty assumption—that the work of Christ terminated with the cross and the empty tomb, rather than continuing in his ascended, heavenly state—has already been questioned by the foregoing observations. It is fundamentally true, of course, that the *atoning* work of Christ has been finished once and for all ("offered for all time one sacrifice for sins" [Heb 10:12]). However, his priestly office continues now in heaven after the ascension, as he intercedes for us ("Christ . . . is at the right hand of God and is also interceding for us" [Rom 8:34]). He is interceding for us that we might enjoy the benefits of his death and resurrection and gift of the Spirit, and one of the chief benefits of his redemption is that we might now experience the *joy* of being in his presence (cf. Ps 16:11; 1 Pet 1:8).

We are now living in union with the One who is interceding for us, seated with him in the heavenly places (Eph 2:6). The practical ways in which these biblical truths of our union with Christ, the presence of the Spirit and our own extended presence with Christ in heaven can inform our practice of biblical meditation will be indicated with some examples below.

PRACTICAL APPLICATION

Meditating by Faith into the Spiritual Senses
Experiencing the Beatific Vision Now

Consider the following examples of experiencing the spiritual senses of Scripture in meditation—one set of examples illustrating the transition from the Old Testament to the New, and the other the transition from the New Testament to the heavenly state. In what follows, the recovery of the spiritual senses is not to be understood as a Procrustean bed into which all texts are forced in some mechanical fashion, but more as a heuristic device, or set of questions that might alert us to the possibility of meanings beyond the literal.

In the Song of Songs the beloved says of her lover, "He has taken me to the banquet hall, / and his banner over me is love" (Song 2:4). It is a well-known fact of church history that from the time of Origen through Bernard of Clairvaux and beyond texts like this in the Song of Songs were understood in a spiritual sense to refer to the love of Christ for his bride, the church.[24]

Biblical interpreters in the modern period have tended to reject such a christological reading, insisting that the literal sense of a celebration of the joys of human love in marriage was the only legitimate one. The traditional spiritual sense, however, has much biblical justification and deserves to be rehabilitated. The apostle Paul, who is quite aware that a text such as Genesis 2:24, "they will become one flesh," refers in its literal sense to human marriage, teaches that in a deeper spiritual sense it points beyond human marriage to "Christ and the church" (Eph 5:32). In the New Testament the church is depicted as the bride of Christ, and the future consummation is spoken of as the "wedding supper of the Lamb" (Rev 19:9). In the new creation marriage will pass away (Mt 22:30), but Christ's love for his bride, the church, will never pass away but rather grow in its depth and fullness forever (cf. Eph 3:18-19). The point in recovering the spiritual sense in meditating on the Song of Songs in the light of Ephesians 5:32 and other New Testament texts with marital imagery is not to deny the literal sense or to reduce the love of Christ for his church to the level of the erotic, but rather to highlight the *joy* in the believer's experience of being loved by Christ. The analogy of human marriage is lifted to a higher level and opens up to us the *affective* dimensions of our relationship with our Savior, which at times can be lost through a disproportionate emphasis on the cognitive and behavioral dimensions of the Christian life.

As another example of finding a spiritual sense in an Old Testament text in the light of the New, consider Psalm 84:1-2:

> How lovely is your dwelling place,
>   O Lord Almighty!
> My soul yearns, even faints,
>   for the courts of the Lord;

---

[24] See Origen, *Commentary on the Song of Songs*, in *The Essential Writings of Christian Mysticism*, pp. 6-12; Bernard of Clairvaux, *On the Song of Songs*, trans. Kilian Walsh (Spencer, Mass.: Cistercian Publications, 1971).

my heart and my flesh cry out
    for the living God.

The psalmist thinks of those who are on pilgrimage (v. 5) to the holy
city and to the temple, and of the joy and satisfaction that he antici-
pates from being near the divine presence in the courts of the Lord
(v. 10). In the new covenant, where the powers of the age to come
(Heb 6:5) have already been inaugurated, we find that the psalmist's
longing can be fulfilled in the worship and believing meditation of
the church. We *have come* to Mount Zion, the heavenly Jerusalem,
and are even now, in an act of true worship, in the presence of a
joyous angelic host and of God and Jesus Christ (Heb 12:22-25).
The architectural beauty of Solomon's temple pales in comparison
with the magnificent beauty and splendor of the new Jerusalem (Rev
21–22), which even now can be seen coming down out of heaven.
In the act of meditation, Psalm 84 can be pondered in the light of
Hebrews 12:22-25, and Hebrews 12:22-25 in turn in conjunction
with Revelation 21–22, as we let the beautiful images of the new
Jerusalem inform and renew our Christian imaginations regarding
the world to come.

A third example illustrates a transition from a New Testament
account of an event in the life of Jesus to the heavenly state: the
transfiguration (Mt 17:1-8; Mk 9:2-8; Lk 9:28-36). In this meditative reading of the transfiguration account, the presence of Peter,
James and John with Jesus on the mountain, and their seeing him
in his glorified state, is seen as pointing to the spiritual state of
the whole church, now seated with the glorified Christ in heaven
("seated . . . in the heavenly realms in Christ Jesus" [Eph 2:6]). This
spiritual and heavenly reality of being in the presence of the glorified Christ in the heavenly realms is an answer to Jesus' prayer
that believers "be with me, where I am, . . . to see my glory" (Jn
17:24). This prayer of Jesus will, of course, be more fully and finally answered at the time of the second coming, when we will

see Christ fully as he is (1 Jn 3:2), when we ourselves will be fully transformed, but even now, *already*, we can begin to see, in the Spirit, his divine glory.

Some commentators on Ephesians 2:6 speak of this being "seated with Christ in the heavenly realms" as a positional truth, presumably in distinction from an actual, experiential truth. While the text does point to a positional truth in the sense of referring to our real relationship with Christ, it should not be limited to such a sense. Being united to Christ, and being raised and seated with him, refers as well to a real state of being and a real experience, by virtue of our connection with the exalted Christ by the Holy Spirit. As Harold Hoehner in his commentary on Ephesians has stated, we are truly "alive in the heavenlies with Christ. . . . This corporate solidarity is a reality now, but in the future its reality will be enlarged as we fully bond with our Savior."[25] And as Thomas Allen has noted in a detailed exegetical study of this text, to be included in Christ's exaltation means to "enter into the corporate person that Christ is"; we are no longer separate individuals but have our own identities, still distinct, but united to his.[26] Where he is, there we are also, being linked to him by the Spirit. Christ's extended self connects him to us; our extended selves are united to his heavenly presence by the Holy Spirit.

The account of the transfiguration can be read not only in the light of Ephesians 2:6 but also in light of another Pauline text, 2 Corinthians 3:18:

> And we, who with unveiled faces all reflect the Lord's glory, are being transformed into his likeness with ever-increasing glory, which comes from the Lord, who is the Spirit.[27]

---

[25] Harold Hoehner, *Ephesians: An Exegetical Commentary* (Grand Rapids: Baker Academic, 2002), p. 336.

[26] Thomas G. Allen, "Exaltation and Solidarity with Christ: Ephesians 1:20 and 2:6," *Journal for the Study of the New Testament* 28 (1986): 110.

[27] The word translated reflect (*katoptrizō*) can also mean "look at in a mirror," but the context here of having the veil removed seems to indicate that "beholding" is the better translation: *ESV Study Bible*, note on 2 Corinthians 3:18, p. 2227.

In the old covenant, Moses went up on Mount Sinai, spent forty days and nights in the presence of God, and came down with his face radiant, glowing with the glory of God (Ex 34:28-35). Paul teaches that in the new covenant all believers can be in the divine presence and experience a more lasting transformation than that experienced by Moses. In his commentary on 2 Corinthians David Garland states it this way:

> Paul asserts that all Christians can, like Moses, approach the glory of the Lord with unveiled faces and experience the same transformation. The emphatic "we all" refers to the experience of all Christians, not just that of apostles or Christian ministers, because Paul is not simply contrasting himself with Moses. . . . Christians are "able to bear the bold, direct revelation of God's glory" because the state of their heart has been changed.[28]

The condition of being "unveiled" or "uncovered" in the glorious, divine presence is a realized, permanent condition brought about by the believer's being justified by God.[29]

This notion of the believer actually being in the divine presence is also supported by another text that has figured prominently in our discussions, Hebrews 12:22-25. In the act of worshiping "in *Spirit* and in truth," we really *are* in the presence of the heavenly, glorified Christ—and for that matter, in the presence of Old Testament saints such as Elijah and Moses, who were with Christ on the mountain. We join with them not on Mount Sinai or on the Mount of Transfiguration, but in the heavenly Zion.

In much of the history of Christian spirituality, the beatific vision has been understood primarily as a future reality; we are "not yet" there in the heavenly state. The thrust of this entire book, and especially the

---

[28]David Garland, *2 Corinthians*, New American Commentary 29 (Nashville: Broadman & Holman, 1999), p. 198.

[29]Jan Lambrecht, *Second Corinthians* (Collegeville, Minn.: Liturgical Press, 1999), p. 55. This realized condition is indicated by the perfect tense of the participle, *anakekalymmenō*, "having been unveiled."

sections on inaugurated eschatology, has been to argue that the believer, in worship and meditation, can begin to experience the beatific vision now: this is the clear implication of texts such as John 17:24, Ephesians 2:6, 2 Corinthians 3:18 and Hebrews 12:22-25. The "not yet" of the Christian pilgrimage must not be allowed to eclipse the reality of the "already."

While it is true that another Pauline text, 1 Corinthians 13:12, reminds us that now, in the "not yet," we only see Christ as in a poor reflection in a mirror—it remains the case that we still can *see Christ*, though only partially. Seeing partially is not the same as not seeing at all!

The seeing in question (2 Cor 3:18) is a spiritual seeing with our spiritual eyes that have been renewed and enlightened by the Holy Spirit (Eph 1:18), but this spiritual seeing is a *real seeing*. As we meditate by faith, in the presence of the Spirit on the text of the transfiguration, in the light of Ephesians 2:6, 2 Corinthians 3:18, Hebrews 12:22-25 and so forth, we can see ourselves seated with Christ (and Peter, James, John, the apostles, Moses, Elijah, the saints and the angels) in the heavenly Jerusalem, beholding his glory and being transformed ourselves by it.

The experience of being transformed may or may not involve at a particular time a sensible awareness of the divine presence or transformation. But just as a patient receiving radiation therapy may not feel, see or taste anything during the radiation treatment, yet later experience a cure from cancer, so it is that the Spirit, influencing our spirit through the biblical text, can do a real work in the soul beyond our conscious awareness. This is the ordinary mysticism of 2 Corinthians 3:18 that is not to be exclusively identified with what are considered to be the more extraordinary mystical states. Meditating by faith on the Scriptures, in the communion of the Holy Spirit, can open up a spiritual horizon—that of Pauline theology and eschatology—in which "all God's children are mystics," in the sense of having a personal experience of real contact, of the presence of Christ and joyful communion with him.

7

Experiencing Communion with God in Biblical Meditation

From Theology to Practice

I**N THE PREVIOUS CHAPTERS** I presented a biblical and systematic theology for an enhanced practice of biblical meditation, focusing on union with Christ, the doctrine of the Trinity and inaugurated eschatology. It is now time to translate this theology into daily practice and to discuss the how-to of biblical meditation. My purpose here is to describe three different levels of biblical meditation: (1) an entry-level practice of meditation ("Getting Started"); (2) as a next step, an intermediate level method of whole-brain or enhanced biblical meditation; and finally (3) a method of worldview meditation or meditation as a way of life: the "Five Practices of Right Comprehension." In the history of Christian spirituality it has sometimes been the custom to distinguish the beginners, the proficients and the perfect (advanced), as to levels of experience and maturity in the Christian life. In those terms, my concern is primarily for those who would consider themselves to be at the beginning and intermediate stages of the Christian pilgrimage.[1]

---

[1]It is not the purpose of this book to give direction as to so-called higher mystical states as described, for example, by St. John of the Cross in *The Dark Night of the Soul* or by St. Teresa of Ávila in the *Interior Castle* (esp. "Mansions," 5-7). The tradition of spirituality advocated in the present essay is in the *kataphatic* rather than the *apophatic* tradition, and seeks to remain clearly

We begin, then, with a discussion of a simple, entry-level method of biblical meditation. The spiritual practice of a slow, prayerful, meditative reading of Scripture has ancient roots in the history of Christianity, as, for example, in the desert spirituality of the Eastern churches. The hermits and anchorites in the deserts of Judea and Egypt would spend many hours of the day and night in prayer and meditation on the Scriptures.[2]

In the third century Origen challenged the monks of the East with a spiritual ideal in which the assiduous study of and meditation on the Scriptures was the mark of genuine conversion. Turning to God meant turning away from the desire for money and riches and worldly fame and glory, and turning to give attention "to the word of God with zeal . . . mind, and care: if we 'meditate on his Law day and night,' if . . . we are exercised in his testimonies, this is to *turn to* the Lord."[3]

In the fourth century St. Pachomius, a pioneer of Egyptian monasticism, required those who entered his monastery to learn by heart—as a *minimum*—the New Testament and the Psalms.[4] In our modern age, as heirs to the printing press and now to the Internet, it is almost beyond our comprehension as Christians that these desert fathers could have memorized so much Scripture, and yet the historical witness that they indeed did so is strong and credible. Their remarkable lives and de-

---

rooted in the biblical texts, doctrines, narratives and imagery. This is not to discount the spiritual depth of these great saints, but I would like to draw attention to a cautionary remark offered by the Vatican's Congregation for the Doctrine of the Faith: "There are certain 'mystical graces' conferred on the founders of ecclesial institutes to benefit their foundation, and on other saints, too, which characterize their personal experience of prayer and which cannot, as such, be the object of imitation and aspiration for other members of the faithful . . . who seek an ever more perfect way of prayer" ("Letter to the Bishops of the Catholic Church on Some Aspects of Christian Meditation," *EWTN*, October 15,1989, www.ewtn.com/library/curia/cdfmed.htm).

In other words, the extraordinary spiritual experiences of great mystics such as Teresa of Ávila and John of the Cross, while instructive for the church, are not necessarily to be considered normative for the experience of all.

[2]For a brief but helpful introduction to the spirituality of the desert fathers, see Benedicta Ward, trans., *The Desert Fathers* (New York: Penguin Books, 2003), pp. vii-xxv. "Though they all knew the Bible by heart [!] and made it the basis of their meditation, the majority could not read or write. . . . [T]hey were not distracted by a learning that stayed with the surface meaning and might encourage them to both possessiveness and boastfulness" (ibid., p. xvii).

[3]Origen, "Exodus Homily XII," in *Homilies on Genesis and Exodus*, trans. Ronald E. Heine (Washington, D.C.: Catholic University of America Press, 1982), pp. 368-69.

[4]Dom Idesbald van Houtryve, *Benedictine Peace* (Westminster, Md.: Newman Press, 1950), p. 135.

votion to the study of the Scriptures stands as an abiding challenge to our own weak memories and short attention spans.

In the sixth century Benedict of Nursia, considered to be one of the chief founders of Western monasticism, carried on many of the spiritual traditions of his predecessors, including the desert fathers and John Cassian (d. 435), and made meditation on Scripture an integral part of his monastic rule. In chapter 48 of his Rule, St. Benedict gives very specific rules for the reading and meditating on Scripture. "Idleness is the enemy of the soul," he stated. "Therefore, all the community must be occupied at definite times in manual labor and at other times in lectio divina."[5] Depending on the time of year, the monks were expected to spend two or three hours in the summertime and as much as five hours a day during the winter to scriptural meditation and spiritual reading.[6]

In the twelfth century the Carthusian monk Guigo II gave explicit articulation to four elements of biblical meditation that had characterized the practice during the preceding centuries (that is, *lectio, meditatio, oratio* and *contemplatio*).[7] *Lectio* is the careful reading of the biblical text (in the ancient church, reading it aloud or hearing it read); *meditatio*, the slow, reflective, leisurely pondering of the words of the text; *oratio* is the responding to God's presence through the text in prayer; and *contemplatio* is the peaceful resting in and enjoyment of the presence of God sensed through the text.[8]

Some authors in the current revival of interest in biblical meditation and contemplative prayer, such as Thomas Keating, have distinguished between earlier monastic and later more scholastic forms of meditation, cautioning that the four elements articulated by Guigo—reading, meditation, prayer and contemplation—should not be understood too

---

[5]*St. Benedict's Rule*, trans. Patrick Barry (Mahwah, N.J.: Hidden Spring, 2004), p. 117.

[6]Wilfrid Tunink, *Vision of Peace: A Study of Benedictine Monastic Life* (New York: Farrer, Straus, 1963), p. 268.

[7]Guigo II, *The Ladder of Monks and Twelve Meditations*, trans. Edmund Colledge and James Walsh (Kalamazoo, Mich.: Cistercian, 1978), cited in Susan Annette Muto, *A Practical Guide to Spiritual Reading* (Petersham, Mass.: St. Bede's Publications, 1994), p. 282.

[8]On these four aspects or elements of *lectio divina* see also Mariano Magrassi, *Praying the Bible: An Introduction to Lectio Divina*, trans. Edward Hagman (Collegeville, Minn.: Liturgical Press, 1998), pp. 103-19. Magrassi was abbot of the Benedictine monastery Santa Maria della Scala, Italy.

rigidly or reduced to a scholastic formula of strictly sequential steps.[9] While Western culture has regarded reading as a purely lineal progression, from start to finish, in biblical meditation, notes John O'Hagan, an American Benedictine monk, "Repetition is crucial. . . . Back and forth, up and down, savoring and balancing what is presently being read with what was recently read."[10]

BIBLICAL MEDITATION
GETTING STARTED

To explain a simple entry-level way of meditating on Scripture, I would like to discuss and then slightly adapt a method formulated by M. Basil Pennington, a Trappist monk at St. Joseph's Abbey in Spencer, Massachusetts. Pennington has been a leader in the post-Vatican II renewal of contemplative prayer, and together with Thomas Keating and others has attempted to bring spiritual practices such as meditating on Scripture from the obscurity of the monasteries into the daily lives of the laity. His method is as follows:

1. Take the Sacred Text with reverence and call upon the Holy Spirit in prayer: e.g., "In your Presence, Lord; Come, Holy Spirit."

2. For ten minutes (or longer, if you are so inclined), listen to the Lord speaking to you through the Text and respond to him in prayer.

3. At the end of the time, choose a word or phrase (perhaps one will have been "given" to you) to take with you, and thank the Lord for being with you, and thank the Lord for being with you and speaking to you.[11]

My slightly adapted version, formulated in terms of four steps, is as follows:

1. Intention and invocation. Form an intention to place yourself in the presence of God; ask for the Holy Spirit to illuminate the text, and

---

[9]Thomas Keating, "The Classical Monastic Practice of Lectio Divina," Contemplative Outreach, October 4, 2008, www.contemplativeoutreach.org/classical-monastic-practice-lectio-divina. Keating notes the later scholastic tendency "to compartmentalize the spiritual life and to rely on rational analysis in theology to the virtual exclusion of personal experience."

[10]John O'Hagan, "Lectio Divina," Monastery of Ascension, www.idahomonks.org/sect810.htm. O'Hagan is a Benedictine monk at the Monastery of the Ascension in southern Idaho.

[11]M. Basil Pennington, "The Method of Lectio," in *Lectio Divina: Renewing the Ancient Practice of Praying the Scriptures* (New York: Crossroad, 1998), p. 151.

to bring you into the presence of Christ: "In your presence, Lord; Come, Holy Spirit."

2. *Reading and reflection.* In a leisurely, prayerful and meditative spirit, spend at least thirty minutes, if possible, in reading the biblical text, slowly pondering its words, images and associations. When beginning to develop a practice of meditation on Scripture, it is probably best in most cases to choose a familiar passage of Scripture such as John 15:5 ("I am the vine; you are the branches. . . . Apart from me you can do nothing") or Matthew 3:13-17, the baptism of Jesus, or Matthew 17:1-8, the transfiguration—a passage that is Christ-centered and easy to visualize. The concrete imagery in such passages makes it refocus our attention when the mind wanders—as it surely will.

3. *Prayer.* Thank God for this time in his presence and for any insights or leading that he may have given you (for example, "Thank you, Lord, for reminding me that in all of my life I am always dependent upon you").

4. *Recollection.* At some later time in the day, remember your time in the presence of the Lord through the text, and remind yourself again of the insight, word, phrase, sense of leading or sense of his presence that you may have experienced during the time of meditation. At the close of the day, perhaps before going to bed, an insight can be recalled (for example, "Thank you, Lord, for reminding me that I, too, am a beloved son of a loving heavenly Father" [having meditated on the baptism of Jesus]).

This is a very simple method for biblical meditation that can be practiced with great benefit in as little as thirty minutes a day. The first step, intention and invocation, is based on the theology of union with Christ and the realized presence of the Holy Spirit, which we discussed in the earlier chapters. In "forming an intention" we are simply acting on the truth that we are really connected and united to Christ by the Holy Spirit as we place ourselves in his presence through the biblical text; we are intentionally realizing and operationalizing our theological convictions. We understand that we are "in Christ"; by faith, we choose to believe that this is true; we intend and form a purpose to be in God's presence; and in our personal prayer and invocation we call on the Holy Spirit to illuminate the text to our hearts and understanding.

The second step, reading and reflection, is at the very heart of biblical meditation. We graze and ruminate on the text in a very leisurely and contemplative manner, having no real agenda other than to be in Christ's presence and *to enjoy* being in Christ's presence. Those of us who are Christian professionals—pastors, priests, seminarians, youth ministers, teachers, academics—often have other agendas as we approach the biblical text: sermons to preach, lessons to be taught, talks to be given, papers to be written. We are data-mining the text for our own purposes, to feed others, while always facing the danger that we will not have first fed ourselves. The wonderful thing about meditating on Scripture is that it is based on the truth that being in the presence of the God who loves us can be the believer's highest joy ("in Your presence *is* fullness of joy [Ps 16:11 NKJV]) and most pleasurable and fulfilling experience. Meditating on the Scriptures by faith, in the Spirit, in a slow and mindful way, is *intrinsically* and not merely *instrumentally* worthwhile. I can honestly say, from my own personal experience, that sensing the presence of God through meditation on the Word, is often the high point of my day, in terms of enjoyment and satisfaction.

If reading and reflection is listening to God, then prayer is our responding to God in light of his presence to us through the text. We thank God for any insight, sense of leading, impressions of his presence, or any word, phrase or thought that has been impressed on us during our time of meditation. What are known as "interior consolations"—particular emotions or impressions of love, joy, peace or the presence of God may *or may not* accompany our time of meditation. It is important to remind ourselves that *God is there even when we do not feel his presence*. Just as a sleeping child can be in her mother's arms and not consciously be aware of the mother's loving presence, so God's presence and love are realities that are not limited to our conscious awareness. Simply *intending* to sincerely place ourselves in the divine presence can have beneficial effects spiritually; the unseen action of the Word and Spirit can benefit our souls apart from noticeable emotion. As Jesus taught in the parable of the growing seed, God can cause the seed of the Word to grow and become fruitful even when we are sleeping, totally unaware of the secret, divine action: "Night and day, whether he [the sower] sleeps or gets up, the seed sprouts and grows, though he does not know how" (Mk 4:27).

The fourth step, recollection, is, strictly speaking, not a part of the meditation time itself, but rather a means of follow-up and take-away. It is helpful for our spiritual growth if we intentionally make the effort to remember at some later time during the same day the insight, word, phrase, image or feeling that might have been impressed upon us during our time of meditation. This could be a spare moment when we are stuck in traffic or waiting in line at the bank or checkout counter. This helps to cement the spiritual benefit that we have received in our souls. Among many biblical examples and precedents of such recollection or remembering, we could think of the virgin Mary, who treasured and pondered in her heart (Lk 2:19) the words spoken about her son Jesus. Since we live today in a media-saturated, overstimulated and information-overloaded environment, it is a good spiritual and cognitive practice to take such a simple step of remembrance and recollection. This simple step can help our brains to transfer the meditative insight from our short-term to our long-term memories, and so make it part of our deeper personal identity.

To illustrate this method for getting started, take as an example Matthew's description of the baptism of Jesus, Matthew 3:13, 16-17:

> Then Jesus came from Galilee to the Jordan to be baptized by John. . . .
> As soon as Jesus was baptized, he went up out of the water. At that moment heaven was opened, and he saw the Spirit of God descending like a dove and lighting on him. And a voice from heaven said, "This is my Son, whom I love; with him I am well pleased."

We first form an intention to place ourselves in the presence of God, reminding ourselves that, as believers, we are already united to Christ by the Holy Spirit as we begin to read and meditate. We ask the Holy Spirit to come and be present to illuminate the text to us. For the next thirty minutes, or longer if possible, we slowly and leisurely read and reflect on the text, using our imaginations to place ourselves in the text, perhaps seeing ourselves first as an observer who may have been on the scene at the time.[12]

---

[12]This method of imagining oneself into the biblical text is a notable feature of Ignatius of Loyola's *Spiritual Exercises* (see "Three Methods of Praying," in *The Spiritual Exercises and Selected Works* [Mahwah, N.J.: Paulist Press, 1991], pp. 420-21). This is not a free use of imagination but imagination that is bounded by the biblical text—in this case, a Gospel story—and as such, subject to Scripture. The point is to engage with the text affectively as well as cognitively, to touch the heart.

We might ponder the fact that all three persons of the Trinity are present in this scene: the Father speaks from heaven; the Son is baptized in the Jordan; the Holy Spirit descends in the form of a dove. The dynamics of the three persons in this earthly scene reflect the heavenly, eternal relationships: the Father has always loved the Son, and the Holy Spirit has been eternally the bond of love between the Father and the Son.

As we reflect on the image of the Holy Spirit in the form of a dove, our minds may be drawn to recall other images of the Holy Spirit: water, wind, fire, oil. The image of the dove may recall the "fluttering, hovering" of the Spirit over the primeval waters of the first creation (Gen 1:2), suggesting the Spirit-over-Jordan waters as a second and new creation, and of Jesus as the second Adam; or perhaps we recall the image of the dove returning to Noah's ark after the flood as a sign of peace, suggestive of the peace experienced by Jesus in the presence of the Father and the Spirit.

As we meditate, we realize that the scene of Jesus' baptism is a beautiful picture of the spiritual realities of our own baptism and sonship through adoption. We too have received the gift of the Holy Spirit, and because of our adoption we too can hear the words spoken to Jesus being spoken to us: "You are my beloved son/daughter; with you I am well pleased." Through our adoption and communion with the Holy Spirit, we are invited into the experience of Jesus' being loved by the Father and his joy in the Holy Spirit by virtue of being loved. Pondering deeply on God's love for us as sons and daughters in Christ makes us grow as happy and joyful Christians.

These reflections are only suggestive, growing out of my own personal experience in meditating on the baptism of Jesus. The point is to spend a good chunk of unhurried time pondering the text and enjoying it, being open to those trains of thought and associations that may be prompted by the Spirit. When our time of meditation is drawing to a close, we thank God in prayer for the insight, image or sense of divine presence that we may have experienced. At some later time of the day, we recollect and remember the insight, image or phrase that has been impressed on us as our spiritual take-away. This, in brief, is how the four steps—intention and invocation, reading and meditation, prayer, and recollection could be applied to a specific biblical text such as the baptism of Jesus.

A question may arise at this point, How do I select a biblical text for my meditation? There is really no one right answer to such a question; I think that the best answer is to choose a biblical text or passage that you feel drawn to at this juncture in your life, and spend a long time—days, weeks, perhaps even longer—and really dig your way deep into the text; let God really write it into the hard drive of your soul. A person feeling very stressed or anxious might be drawn to Psalm 23; someone seeking a more intimate relationship with Christ could be drawn to John 15 and the imagery of "abiding in the vine," and so forth.

As I mentioned earlier, years ago I was drawn to the first chapter of Ephesians, spent over six months meditating on this great Pauline text, and found it to be a wonderfully enjoyable and transformative experience. Currently I have been drawn to John 17, Jesus' high priestly prayer and his heart for the unity of believers in the church as a sign of God's love for believers, and that Jesus was truly sent by the Father. More recently, I have been meditating on the tenth chapter of the book of Hebrews, on how the perfect, finished atoning work of Christ on the cross (Heb 10:14) gives us the assurance that now we can experience closeness to God ("Let us draw near to God . . . in full assurance of faith" [Heb 10:22]).

However, that being said, it remains the case that many people will desire some more systematic plan for reading and meditating on Scripture. There are many plans available for those who would like to read through the whole sweep of Scripture on some regular basis. For example, the English Standard Version (esv) website (www.esv.org/biblereadingplans) lists a variety of daily reading plans, including the M'Cheyne One-Year Reading Plan (daily Old Testament, New Testament, and Psalms or Gospels), a chronological reading plan, and the lectionary readings from the Book of Common Prayer Daily Office (daily Psalms, Old Testament, New Testament, and Gospel).[13] The ad-

---

[13]Many of the major denominations provide their own Bible reading plans, e.g., Presbyterian Church USA (http://gamc.pcusa.org/ministries/devotions/); Evangelical Lutheran Church in

vantage of the lectionary cycle from the Book of Common Prayer Daily Office is that the readings are keyed to the church year and give regular exposure to the great events in the life of Christ: his birth, ministry, death, resurrection, ascension and sending of the Holy Spirit.

I personally try to combine the lectionary readings with meditating on a particular text to which I am drawn at a given time, but there really are no one-size-fits-all rules here. The important thing is to simply spend as much time as you can in leisurely, prayerful pondering of the text.

A few words need to be said about the practicalities of biblical meditation, especially concerning time, place and personal disposition. Historically, many Christians have found the early morning hours the best time for prayer. We are told in Mark 1:35 that "Very early in the morning, while it was still dark, Jesus got up, left the house and went off to a solitary place, where he prayed." Early in the morning we may feel fresher and have more energy to bring to God and fewer distractions and interruptions. However, many have found that other times of the day, perhaps in the evenings before going to bed, to be better times for reflection, meditation and prayer. Your own biorhythms and knowledge of your own circumstances and temperament are the best guides in such matters.

The place for our practice of meditation is important; it is essential to have a space which is quiet and where we can feel free from unnecessary interruption, and where we can have a sense of privacy and intimacy in our time with God. If possible, it is desirable to have a "dedicated" room or space that is exclusively or primarily used for our devotional time, perhaps with some religious symbols or artwork that reinforce the special sense of a sacred space. A comfortable chair is helpful—but not so comfortable that we are tempted to fall asleep! Having our Bible and other devotional readings close at hand and readily accessible makes it easier to transition into our devotional reading of Scripture without unnecessary loss of time.

America (www.elca.org/What-We-Believe/The-Bible/Read-the-Bible/Read-the-Bible-in-One-Year.aspx); Greek Orthodox Archdiocese of America (www.goarch.org/resources/monthly_readings); Roman Catholic: official texts of the daily Mass, in *Magnificat* (www.magnificat.net/english). See also the *One Year Bible Online* at (www.oneyearbibleonline.com).

Other preparatory matters relate to our inner dispositions and states of the heart as we come to our time of prayer and meditation. Michael Casey has spoken of the problem of "inner noise," the chatter and static that is constantly buzzing in our heads as we live in our rushed, over-stimulated and media-saturated worlds. "The largest obstacle that prevents our hearing the word of God is the volume of interior noise that interferes with our perception," he notes. "Even when we slow down and cease from other activities, we do not easily enter into a state of expectant listening."[14]

Of late, in light of this problem of inner noise, I have begun to change my earlier habit of listening to talk radio when driving in the car, deciding instead to turn it off and ride in silence, reflecting on the issues of the day or recollecting an insight or thought that may have arisen during my time of meditation. We have only so much shelf space in our minds, and with so many stimuli competing for our attention, it is a good cognitive and spiritual practice to be a bit more mindful and intentional about our own streams of consciousness and what we are choosing to feed those streams.

The University of Chicago psychologist Mihaly Csikszentmihalyi has estimated that over a lifetime of seventy years, a human being, awake and aware for sixteen hours a day, could process about (only) 185 billion bits of information.[15] The mind's "carrying capacity," though seemingly vast, is limited, and we are wise to be very careful in how we choose to fill the shelf spaces of our minds. Otherwise, the good seed of the Word will be choked out by the thorns and thistles (Mk 4:7) of all the ambient noise of our busy lives and will not be fruitful.

Another factor that can interfere with the calm and relaxed disposition that we need for our times of meditation is the feeling of being *rushed* and stressed out by our busy, overscheduled lives.[16] Our daily

---

[14]Michael Casey, *Sacred Reading: The Ancient Art of Lectio Divina* (Liguori, Mo.: Liguori Books, 1995), p. 94.

[15]Mihaly Csikszentmihalyi, *Flow: The Psychology of Optimal Experience* (New York: HarperCollins, 1990), p. 33. He observes that "Each person allocates his or her limited attention either by focusing it intentionally like a beam of energy . . . or by diffusing it in desultory, random movements. The shape and content of life depend on how attention has been used. . . . Attention is our most important tool in the task of improving the quality of experience" (ibid., p. 33).

[16]The Slow Movement that emerged during the 1990s—slow food, slow travel, slow reading

to-do lists are not far from our minds even as we try to pray. The Bene-dictine monastic Hubert Van Zeller has noted that "Nothing so de-stroys the prayerfulness of spiritual study as rush and fuss. Tension is the enemy of meditation as St. Benedict conceived it."[17]

There is, of course, no magic bullet to solve the problem of feeling rushed even as we try to pray and read. We can, however, remind our-selves as we begin, *This time is really important to me, and to God; as im-portant or more important than the things on my to-do list; I am in the will of God by doing this.* A friend of mine in church suggested a little prayer in this regard that I have found personally helpful: "God, you know what I need to do this day; please take care of those tasks, issues, worries and people that I am concerned about during this time that I want to spend with you." Like handing over our coats to the attendant at the coat room at a museum or hotel, so that we can be less encumbered for the event, we can hand over our concerns to God for a time, and then return to them later.[18]

Even having taken such steps, the experience of the ages, even among the most "advanced" saints of God, has been that our minds will still wander and be distracted as we try to focus our attention on God as we meditate and pray. Rather than inflicting needless feelings of guilt on ourselves, it is a better strategy simply to *notice* that we have been distracted, and then to bring our attention back to God and to the text—as often as we need to. It is a waste of our limited psychic energy to beat up ourselves for our failures of attention; simply bring back our attention to God. A basketball player who has committed a needless foul will not help himself or teammates by berating himself or the referee; he needs to keep his eyes on the ball and keep focused on the game. I

---

etc.—was a pushback on the increasing speed and rush of contemporary life. See Carl Honore, *In Praise of Slowness: Challenging the Cult of Speed* (New York: HarperCollins, 2004). The point here is not that everything should literally be done slowly but rather be done at the right and appropriate speed; some things—friendship, wisdom and worship—for example, take time to cultivate and enjoy. See also John Miedema, *Slow Reading* (Duluth, Minn.: Litwin Books, 2009). Biblical meditation is, of course, an ancient practice of slow reading.

[17]Dom Hubert Van Zeller, *The Holy Rule: Notes on St. Benedict's Legislation for Monks* (New York: Sheed & Ward, 1958), p. 306.

[18]Please do not misunderstand the illustration: God, of course, is not just a coatroom atten-dant—he is the main event!

use a simple breath prayer—"In your presence, Lord"—to *refocus* my attention and to *renew* my intention to be in God's presence.

These distractions are not the only barriers, of course, to fruitful meditation: there are even more important spiritual issues that affect the state of our hearts. Jesus teaches us that "Blessed are the pure in heart, for they will see God" (Mt 5:8). We need to purify our hearts from the sins and defilements that cloud our vision of God and hinder our fellowship with Christ. We need to purify our hearts by confessing our sins to God before we can expect to have enjoyable communion with him.[19] Likewise, if we are upset by broken relationships (cf. Mt 5:23-24) or anger or depression, we need to deal with these problems before we can enjoy fruitful times in God's presence. We may need to seek pastoral or professional help, or the help of a support group, to deal with seemingly chronic issues that are beyond our personal resources to resolve—but such is the way of wisdom in order to keep seeking the "pearl of great price."

EXCURSUS
CENTERING PRAYER, THE JESUS PRAYER, FOCUSING PRAYER

In this excursus I would like to comment on two forms of contemplative prayer—Centering Prayer and the Jesus Prayer—that are becoming more widely known and practiced in many American churches, including Protestant and evangelical churches. (Some readers may wish to skip this section and proceed directly to the next section on Whole-Brain Meditation.) Neither, strictly speaking, are forms of the type of biblical meditation that has been explained in this book, but rather forms of contemplative prayer that can be practiced for their own sake or as training exercises that strengthen the mind's ability to stay focused on and attentive to God.

Both Centering Prayer, rooted in the Roman Catholic tradition, and the Jesus Prayer, rooted in the Eastern Orthodox tradition, attempt to

---

[19]A classic prayer from the Book of Common Prayer, the "Collect for Purity," is a good one to use both in relation to personal confession and the illuminating presence of the Holy Spirit: "Almighty God, unto whom all hearts are open, all desires known, and from whom no secrets are hid: Cleanse the thoughts of our hearts by the inspiration of your Holy Spirit, that we may perfectly love thee, and worthily magnify thy holy name; through Christ our Lord, Amen."

provide two spiritual benefits to their practitioners: a sense of direct communion with God and a meditative technique that can help focus the mind on God in the midst of the overstimulation and distractions of our modern digital environment. It is my purpose, after giving a brief theological and historical assessment of these forms of contemplative prayer, to propose an alternative, Focusing Prayer, that provides such benefits while at the same time may be more suitable to a Protestant evangelical spirituality rooted in the verbal revelation of Scripture and the doctrines of creation, incarnation and atonement.

Centering Prayer in its contemporary form was developed in the 1970s by Thomas Keating, a Cistercian monk and former abbot of St. Joseph's Abbey in Spencer, Massachusetts. Keating was building on the earlier efforts of his friend Father William Meninger, who had retrieved the mystical method of prayer in the fourteenth-century work *The Cloud of Unknowing* and had begun to teach it to priests in retreat settings.[20] Keating was concerned that at this time (the 1970s) many Roman Catholics who were seeking a deeper experience of God were turning to Buddhist and Hindu meditative practices, believing that their own Christian and Catholic churches had little to offer in the way of specific guidance. Centering Prayer, which involves the quiet, reflective and repetitive use of a single word, such as *God* or *love* or another personally meaningful word or phrase, was intended to help fill this spiritual vacuum. The practice is based on the theological truth of the indwelling presence of the three persons of the Trinity in the soul (cf. Jn 14:16-23). The purpose of Centering Prayer is to keep the intention and attention focused on God, so that the mind is quieted and still, resting in God, and not working discursively with thoughts, concepts and images.[21] The method of Centering Prayer was widely received in Catholic circles and beyond, and is now being propagated through the work of the organization Contemplative Outreach and its

---

[20]See Thomas Keating, "The Origins of Centering Prayer," in *Intimacy with God* (New York: Crossroad, 1994), pp. 11-22; James Walsh, ed., *The Cloud of Unknowing* (Mahwah, N.J.: Paulist Press, 1981), with extensive introduction, pp. 1-97.

[21]Keating, "Will and Intention in Centering Prayer," "The Sacred Symbol as a Gesture of Consent," and "The Psychology of Centering Prayer," in ibid., chaps. 6-8.

sponsored workshops, retreats, publications and teaching events.[22]

The Jesus Prayer ("Lord Jesus Christ, Son of God, have mercy on me, a sinner") has its roots in the ancient traditions of the Eastern church. This ancient prayer with its four elements—devotion to the name of Jesus, sorrow for sin, frequent repetition and an imageless, nondiscursive tendency leading to inner silence, emerged as a practical method with Diadochus of Photice (5th cent.), and was also commended by St. John Climacus (7th cent.) in his *Ladder of Divine Ascent*.[23] In the thirteenth century Nicephorus, a monk of Mount Athos, recommended that the prayer be said with the chin resting on the chest and the gaze focusing on the navel, so as to focus inwardly on the heart. In the fourteenth century the practice of this prayer was defended by St. Gregory Palamas against the attacks of the philosopher Barlaam of Calabria.[24] Palamas defended the monks' conviction that through the prayer they indeed were experiencing in some real sense direct communion with God and were seeing a vision of the uncreated light of God. Palamas drew a distinction between the energies and essence of God, arguing that while the essence of God remained radically unknowable, the energies of God were accessible to Christian experience in creation and the depths of the soul.

In the eighteenth century the hesychast movement and Jesus Prayer experienced something of a renaissance with the publication of the *Philokalia*, a collection of patristic and later texts from the Eastern church, translated into the languages of other Orthodox and Western churches.[25] This work, together with the popular nineteenth-century

---

[22]See Contemplative Outreach's website at www.contemplativeoutreach.org.

[23]Ronald J. Zawilla, "Hesychasm," in *The New Dictionary of Catholic Spirituality*, ed. Michael Downey (Collegeville, Minn.: Liturgical Press, 1993), pp. 471-73. This article is a very concise and helpful survey of the hesychast ("quiet, stillness") movement and the history of the Jesus Prayer, and I have followed it in my account.

[24]Ibid., p. 472. For further discussion of the Jesus Prayer, see also Vladimir Lossky, "The Way of Union," and "The Divine Light," in *The Mystical Theology of the Eastern Church* (Crestwood, N.Y.: St. Vladimir's Seminary Press, 1976), pp. 209-34; *The Way of a Pilgrim*, trans. Helen Bacovcin (Garden City, N.J.: Doubleday, 1978); E. Kadloubovsky and G. E. H. Palmer, trans., *Writings from the Philokalia on Prayer of the Heart* (London: Faber, 1951); and Kallistos Ware, "The Hesychasts: Gregory of Sinai, Gregory of Palamas, Nicolas Cabasilas" and "The Hesychast Renaissance," in *The Study of Spirituality*, ed. C. Jones, G. Wainwright and E. Yarnold (New York: Oxford University Press, 1986), pp. 242-58.

[25]Zawilla, "Hesychasm," p. 473.

work *The Way of a Pilgrim*, led to the growing awareness and practice of the Jesus Prayer down to the present day.[26]

Several observations are in order with respect to Centering Prayer and the Jesus Prayer, especially in regard to three issues: the use of repetition in the prayers, the historical connections with Neo-Platonism and the apophatic tradition in Christian spirituality, and the distinctiveness of these methods in relation to Eastern and other non-Christian methods of prayer. These comments are in no way meant to suggest that those who practice these methods of prayer have not in fact experienced genuine communion with God or derived great personal spiritual benefits.

Evangelical Protestants tend to be wary of the repetitive, seemingly mantra-like quality of the Jesus and Centering prayers, recalling Jesus' warning against the vain repetition of the pagans (cf. Mt 6:7). However, there is biblical warrant to recognize the fact that repetition in prayer and worship is not inherently problematic: the living creatures before the throne of God day and night *never stop saying:* "Holy, holy, holy is the Lord God Almighty, who was, and is, and is to come" (Rev 4:8). Repetition can be vain if it is insincere or designed to impress people or manipulate God; here the living creatures are doing that which is eminently appropriate, acknowledging the holiness, majesty and greatness of God. It is the intention and purpose of the repetition, not the fact of repetition itself, that determines its spiritual value. Of course, any repetitive prayer or liturgical practice can become mechanical and rote, and can stand in need of being refreshed by an intentional recollection and self-reminder of the purpose of what one is doing or saying.

Another question that arises from an evangelical Protestant perspective concerns the primary focus and tendency of the Jesus Prayer: "Lord Jesus Christ, Son of God, have mercy on me (a sinner)." The question here is whether the words of the prayer, constantly repeated, adequately reflect the biblical doctrines of the atonement, adoption and

---

[26]As an indication of the interest in the Jesus Prayer and Orthodox forms of spirituality in evangelical circles, one might note the favorable reception of Frederica Matthewes-Green at her convocation lecture on "Orthodoxy and Evangelical Renewal" at Gordon College in March of 2009. See also her book *The Jesus Prayer: The Ancient Desert Prayer that Tunes the Heart to God* (Brewster, Mass.: Paraclete Press, 2009). A former Episcopalian, Green converted, along with her husband, to Orthodoxy in 1993.

the "already" dimensions of New Testament eschatology. Humility before God and dependence on divine mercy is always in order, of course, but at the same time, the writer of the epistle to the Hebrews, out of a deep conviction of the power of the finished atoning work of Christ, encourages us to have *confidence* "to enter the Most Holy Place by the blood of Jesus" and to "draw near to God with a sincere heart in *full assurance* of faith" (Heb 10:19, 22, emphasis added). This confidence, based on a clear biblical understanding of the sufficiency of the atonement, has been a hallmark of classic Reformation theology and should continue to be clearly held and practiced as evangelical Protestants continue to interact with Orthodox and Roman Catholic Christians and their traditions of spirituality. The comments that are being offered here are not for the purpose of *recommending* the use of the Jesus Prayer or Centering Prayer for evangelical Protestants, but rather, to give some historical and theological context for understanding these other practices—within the larger purpose of this book—which is to recommend the practices of biblical meditation as here set forth.

Similarly, the crucial New Testament truth of adoption—that we, through faith and the work of the Spirit, are sons and daughters of God, crying *"Abba,* Father" (Rom 8:15; Gal 4:6-7)—is foundational for Christian identity and spirituality. Though we continue to *sin,* our fundamental identify before God is not that of *sinner* or *servant* (though both are still true in a relative and circumstantial sense), but rather that of a beloved *son* or *daughter.* We have been raised with Christ, seated with him in the heavenly places, blessed with every spiritual blessing in the heavenly places (Eph 1:3), and even now have already begun to see the glory of God shining in the face of Jesus Christ (2 Cor 3:18; 4:6). As beloved sons and daughters of God, we know ourselves to be loved by God our Father, knowing that "there is now no condemnation for those who are in Christ Jesus" and that we have been set free from the law of sin and death (Rom 8:1-2).

The historical connections of both Centering Prayer and the Jesus Prayer with Neo-Platonism are important questions to consider. The influence of the Neo-Platonic writings of Pseudo-Dionysius the Areopagite on both Eastern and Western Christian spirituality has been enormous.

Dionysius the Areopagite was believed for most of church history to be the convert of St. Paul mentioned in Acts 17 and the first bishop of Athens.[27] According to Harvey Egan, a leading scholar of the history and theology of mysticism, this "benign imposter," who claimed to have been a disciple of Paul, to have been with the apostles Peter and James when the virgin Mary died, and to have corresponded with John the Evangelist, was not "outed" until the nineteenth century; contemporary scholars now conjecture that he was in fact a sixth-century Syrian monk.[28]

The works of Pseudo-Dionysius were translated from the Greek into Latin in the ninth century by the Irish philosopher and theologian John Scotus Erigena. In the fourteenth century the influence of the Areopagite was further disseminated through the anonymous author of *The Cloud of Unknowing* in England.[29] Pseudo-Dionysius's apophatic spirituality introduced the notions of the absolute Godhead as the "Divine Dark," the "negation of all that *is*," and the soul's attainment of union with God as "divine ignorance."[30] These notions are, for example, reflected in a text such as *The Mystical Theology*, "The Divine Dark":

And you, beloved Timothy,
In the earnest exercise of mystical contemplation abandon
all sensation and
all intellection and
all objects or sensed
or seen and
all being and
all nonbeing and
in unknowing, as much as may be, be
one with the beyond being and knowing. By the ceaseless and
limitless going out of yourself and

---

[27]Harvey Egan, "Pseudo-Dionysius," in *An Anthology of Christian Mysticism* (Collegeville, Minn.: Liturgical Press, 1991), p. 91.

[28]Ibid., p. 91. Egan notes that Pseudo-Dionysius's writings "attained almost canonical status— at least in the Western medieval world. . . . His sharp distinction between apophatic and kataphatic theology paved the way for the later split between mystical experience of God and faith seeking understanding" (ibid., pp. 91, 95).

[29]Evelyn Underhill, *Mysticism* (London: Methuen, 1962), pp. 457, 459.

[30]Ibid., p. 457. Underhill notes here that such ideas, "common to Greek and Indian philosophy," with Dionysius "enter the Catholic fold."

out of all things else you will be led in utter pureness,
rejecting all and released from all,
aloft to the flashing forth,
beyond all being, of the divine dark.[31]

Such an apophatic and negative theology is problematic from the perspective of a Reformational and evangelical theology, if taken without
substantial correction and modification. While it is certainly true that
human words and thoughts can never *exhaust* the knowledge of the
infinite God, the words of Scripture are nevertheless given to us that
we can know God *truly* and analogically, in a way proportionate to
and appropriate to our human finitude. Linguisticality is not an accidental property of God but inherent in God's eternal being (cf. Jn
1:1, "In the beginning was the *Logos*"). Believers are to be sanctified by
the truth of God, given to us in the form of words given to Jesus by the
Father (Jn 17:8, 17), and revealed by and inspired by the Holy Spirit
(1 Cor 2:13).[32] The fact of the incarnation means that even now in
heaven, and into eternity, the historical Jesus will have a definite,
though glorified, bodily form, which is properly imaged in Scripture
and Christian experience. For all eternity the glorified Jesus will still
have a human nature and consequently a human experience of the
knowledge of God—a knowledge of God that of course transcends our
knowledge, but is not *utterly dissimilar* to it. By leaving words and
images behind, an exclusively apophatic style of meditation tends to
erase the boundaries between Eastern (Buddhist, Hindu) and Christian
forms of meditation. Studies conducted in the summer of 1999 by Dr.
Andrew Newberg, a neuroscientist at the University of Pennsylvania,
did in fact find that the neurological changes detected in Catholic nuns
practicing Centering Prayer were nearly the same as those detected in
Buddhist meditators, despite the very different belief systems.[33]

---

[31]In Egan, "Pseudo-Dionysius," p. 97.

[32]In his fine study of the terminology of biblical meditation, Walter Kaiser demonstrates that
the biblical writers, when discussing meditation, focus on the words of God in the law of God,
the mighty acts of God in creation and redemption, and the attributes of God so revealed. See
Walter C. Kaiser, "What Is Biblical Meditation?" in *Renewing Your Mind in a Secular World*,
ed. John D. Woodbridge (Chicago: Moody Press, 1985), pp. 39-53.

[33]Andrew Newberg and Mark Robert Waldman, "Comparing the Centering Prayer to Buddhist

If in Neo-Platonism the movement of spiritual liberation and union with the Absolute is from matter to pure spirit, in New Testament theology salvation is a movement from unredeemed matter and the body and mind to *redeemed* and glorified matter and the body and mind—to a new *creation* (Rev 21–22; Rom 8:21-22). The predominant thrust of Pauline spirituality is not so much inward as it is upward and outward to experience and realize our true situation as being raised with Christ and seated with him in the heavenly realms (Eph 2:6). "Since, then, you have been raised with Christ, set your hearts *on things above.* . . . Set your minds *on things above,* not on earthly things" (Col 3:1-2, emphasis added). Set your minds: don't leave them behind.

The movement in New Testament spirituality is not toward a darkness but a movement toward the *light:* the glory and light of God shining in the face of Christ (2 Cor 3:18; 4:6), and the glorious brilliance of the new Jerusalem, which needs not the light of the sun, because the Lamb of God is its light (Rev 21:23).

Suffice it to say that there is good biblical warrant to conclude that Christian spirituality should not appeal to Pseudo-Dionysius or to a Neo-Platonic metaphysics to seek communion with God. The wonderful truths of the incarnation, the atonement, adoption, the gift of the Holy Spirit and union with Christ are the robust biblical foundations of our enjoyment of communion with God through the Scriptures.

I suggest, then, as an alternative to both Centering and the Jesus Prayer a form of Focusing Prayer that can, I believe, provide the spiritual benefits sought in those other forms of contemplative prayer, but with biblical and theological foundations more in keeping with Protestant and evangelical sensibilities. One form of such a focusing prayer that could be practiced is based on the following words, rooted in Psalm 103:1-5, and as paraphrased and adapted in a Taizé song and melody:

Bless the Lord, O my soul, and bless God's holy name;
Bless the Lord, O my soul, who leads me into life. (repeat)

Meditation," in *How God Changes Your Brain* (New York: Ballantine Books, 2009), pp. 48-49. "Frontal lobe activity increases, limbic activity decreases, and the combination generates a peaceful and serene state of consciousness" (ibid.).

This form of prayer—not as a substitute for biblical meditation, but as a preparatory exercise or supplement—is a worthwhile spiritual exercise for a number of reasons, including the fact that it is both biblical in its content and consistent with our chief human purpose, "To glorify God and to enjoy him forever" (Westminster Shorter Catechism, Q.1). Offering these words to God in rhythmic, prayerful fashion is a way of praising God in gratitude and thanksgiving for all the great benefits of salvation. Rather than using merely a single word (*Jesus, love* or *God*), a longer text of Scripture can connect the mind with the larger biblical narrative and the history of redemption.

One could use many other biblical texts that are personally meaningful in similar fashion. Such a focusing prayer helps to focus and calm the mind and train our attentiveness, and can easily be used during odd moments in the day, when we may be standing in line or waiting for an appointment.[34] One could use this method when exercising at the gym or walking for exercise. When your attention wanders—as it surely will—you can recall your intention to be in the presence of Christ with the words, "In your presence, Lord," and continue the time of focusing meditation.

THE NEXT STEP
WHOLE-BRAIN MEDITATION

The next step to an intermediate level of meditation is a method that I call whole-brain meditation. In this method a propositional text, say from an epistle, such as Romans 5:5, "God has poured out his love into our hearts by the Holy Spirit, whom he has given us," is paired with a pictorial or narrative text, such as the baptism of Jesus (Mt 3:13-17), in a way that will be further explained.

The method of whole-brain meditation is premised on current research in cognitive science and educational psychology related to brain lateralization and dual-coding theories of learning and memory. Most people are now familiar with the concept of differing *left brain* and *right*

---

[34]Such contemplative meditation has been shown by neuroscientific research to have health and cognitive benefits, including positive effects on cognition, relaxation and psychological health (ibid., p. 159).

brain ways of thinking. More precisely, in cognitive psychology and neuroscience this phenomenon is known as brain *lateralization*. Research by cognitive psychologists has shown that most people (about 95 percent) show a specialization for language in the left hemisphere of the brain, whereas the right hemisphere is thought to be focused on the integration of visual and spatial information.[35] One should not overstate the left-right brain distinction, of course, since the two hemispheres of the brain are connected, but the fact of lateralization does suggest that methods of Bible study and meditation that reach the whole brain would be preferable to those that activate primarily one hemisphere.[36]

Many educational psychologists today work with dual-coding theories of learning and memory. Brain scan studies have demonstrated that different areas of the brain are activated by pictures as compared to words alone in comprehension and memory tests; our brains apparently contain different modules for processing different types of stimuli and are accessed by different neural pathways.[37] Cerebral blood-flows to different parts of the brain can be tracked as subjects perform different memory tasks; strong activation was found in the occipital lobe and posterior regions for subjects processing visual stimuli, but not while processing arithmetic or auditory stimuli.[38]

Building on this research in neuroscience and cognitive psychology, educational psychologists have developed dual-coding theories of learning that postulate that human beings have separate channels for processing visual and auditory information, and that learning is more effective when students process information with both channels of the brain rather than either one alone. Empirical research has in fact

---

[35]Kathleen M. Galotti, *Cognitive Psychology*, 4th ed. (Belmont, Calif.: Thomson Wadsworth, 2008), pp. 46-47.

[36]Similar considerations would apply to homiletics and effective preaching. For a very helpful and insightful article on whole-brain preaching see Allen Nauss, "Preaching Sermons That Will Be Remembered: Unleashing the Spirit's Power in the Brain," *Concordia Journal* 34, no. 4 (2008): 264-91, with extensive bibliography and citations of literature in neuroscience and cognitive psychology.

[37]Allen Paivio, *Mind and Its Evolution: A Dual-Coding Theoretical Interpretation* (Mahwah, N.J.: Lawrence, Erlbaum, 2006), chap. 8; and Allen Paivio and W. Lambert, "Dual Coding and Bilingual Memory," *Journal of Verbal Learning & Verbal Behavior* 20 (1981): 532-39.

[38]Galotti, *Cognitive Psychology*, p. 324.

demonstrated that learning comprehension and retention is improved when pictures are added to words, when a text is placed in close proximity to the corresponding graphic, and when extraneous material is eliminated.[39]

The application of this research to our practice of biblical meditation is very straightforward: in our meditation on Scripture, we intentionally try to combine words and concepts with concrete images and narratives. A propositional text is paired with one or more pictorial or narrative texts that share a common theme. For example, to cite some texts that have appeared earlier in this book, Matthew's account of the baptism of Jesus (Mt 3:13-17) can be paired with texts in Paul that deal with *sonship* (Rom 8:15-17; Gal 3:26; 4:6-7) and with the parable of the father's love for his returning prodigal son (Lk 15:11-32):

> As soon as Jesus was baptized, he went up out of the water. At that moment heaven was opened, and he saw the Spirit of God descending like a dove and lighting on him. And a voice from heaven said, "This is my Son, whom I love; with him I am well pleased." (Mt 3:16-17)

> God has poured out his love into our hearts by the Holy Spirit, whom he has given us. (Rom 5:5)

> For you did not receive a spirit that makes you a slave again to fear, but you have received the Spirit of sonship. And by him we cry, *"Abba,* Father." The Spirit himself testifies with our spirit that we are God's children. (Rom 8:15-16)

> You are all sons of God through faith in Christ Jesus. . . .
> Because you are sons, God sent the Spirit of his Son into our hearts, the Spirit who calls out *"Abba,* Father." (Gal 3:26; 4:6)

---

[39]This extensive, laboratory-based educational research is summarized in Richard E. Mayer, "Multi-Media Principle," in *Multi-Media Learning*, 2nd ed. (New York: Cambridge University Press, 2009), pp. 223-41, esp. p. 240. "The multi-media principle is perhaps the most fundamental principle of multimedia design: Present words and pictures rather than words alone. . . . The research presented in this chapter demonstrates that educators should consider ways to incorporate graphics into their lessons. . . . [T]he main implication for instruction is that a words-only lesson can be improved by adding appropriate graphics." Mayer is professor of psychology at University of California, Santa Barbara, and a leading researcher in the field of educational psychology and learning theory.

He got up and went to his father.

But while he was still a long way off, his father saw him and was filled with compassion for him; he ran to his son, threw his arms around him and kissed him. (Lk 15:20)

Meditating on these texts together can have a greater impact on the heart than a single text in isolation. The Pauline texts state the wonderful gospel truth of our adoption and sonship; the other texts help us to understand and experience what sonship *looks like* and *feels like* at a very personal level. Like the parables of Jesus, this method connects a concept (the kingdom of God) with concrete images (yeast, a lamp, a treasure buried in a field, a pearl of great price), and as a result we are much more likely to remember the biblical teaching.

In the case of the texts cited, as we meditate on the baptism of Jesus and hear the Father's words to Jesus ("my beloved Son, with whom I am well pleased"), we realize, in the light of the other texts, that *we* are beloved sons and daughters of the Father, and that the Holy Spirit has poured the love of God into our hearts, so that the Father's love for Jesus is the great illustration of God's love for us. Our salvation is our participation in Jesus' joyous experience of being loved and accepted—in time and eternity—by the Father, in the communion of the Holy Spirit. The advantage of this whole-brain method of meditation is that the pictures and narratives help us to feel our way into the texts and to experience them at the emotional as well as the cognitive levels,[40] and so experience communion with God and joy in him at a deeper level. Since we really *are* united to Christ by the Holy Spirit, and since the Holy Spirit *really* does illuminate the biblical text, the text can come alive to us at the experiential level—as the text was meant to be.

As to the potentially powerful and spiritually beneficial impact of such a whole-brain type of meditation, consider the following report

---

[40]Nauss cites neuroscience research that shows which metaphors and stories, which connect with the emotions, are more likely to be cemented in the memory than abstract concepts alone: "To ensure memory persistence, it would appear to be effective to identify the emotions that are part of a sermon text and then to find metaphors and stories that reflect those feelings" ("Preaching Sermons That Will Be Remembered," p. 274). Compare also James McGaugh, *Memory and Emotion* (New York: Columbia University Press, 2003), pp. 117-61, cited in Nauss.

by a seminary student, "J," of his experience of meditating on the
baptism of Jesus:

> I found Mt 3:17 to be particularly powerful. My father died when I
> was nine; my relationship with my father was not too good. Although
> my father was not necessarily a bad father, some images had been left
> in my mind that give me a negative impression of father figures.
> During the fifteen years before coming to seminary I worked in a
> highly competitive corporate sales setting . . . my success brought
> great stress. I felt that the stress was partially due to my deep hunger
> for acceptance and acknowledgement. Reading Mt 3:17, I pictured the
> scene and heard the Father's voice communicating unconditional ac-
> ceptance to his Son, before Jesus has even begun his ministry! I felt
> moved by that incredible approbation, and struggled between the
> negative image of my earthly father and the positive image of my
> heavenly Father. . . .
>
> I have found that many men and women have had similar negative
> experiences with earthly fathers, so it is now my passion to introduce to
> them the glorious heavenly Father.[41]

J's experience shows that such whole-brain meditation, empowered by
the Spirit and faith, can be part of a process of the healing of memories
and a step toward a more intimate and loving experience with our
heavenly Father.[42]

As a second example, consider a pairing of an Old Testament text
from the prophets (Zeph 3:14-15, 17) with a text from a New Testament epistle (Heb 12:22-25), both dealing with themes related to the
good news of the gospel and the joyful experience of being in the
presence of God as the result of our salvation experience:

---

[41]The student's report was originally narrated as though speaking in the third person; this has
been translated into a first-person voice for clarity of understanding.

[42]Neuroscientific research on memory shows that the neuroplasticity of the brain, allowing
it to rewire itself in the light of new experience, can reframe our memories and remove
some of the negative emotional impact of past traumatic events. See Curt Thomson, *Anatomy of the Soul* (Carrollton, Tex.: SaltRiver, 2010), p. 73. "The good news is that you do not
have to remain in the morass of your implicit memory. . . . Despite the fact that you cannot
turn back the clock and change the actual events of your life, *you can change the experience of
what you remember and so change your memory*" (ibid.). Thompson is a practicing psychiatrist
and evangelical Christian.

Sing, O Daughter of Zion. . . .

Be glad and rejoice with all your heart. . . .

The LORD has taken away your punishment. . . .

The LORD your God is with you,
    he is mighty to save.

He will take great delight in you,
    he will quiet you with his love,
    he will *rejoice over you with singing.*
    (Zeph 3:14-15, 17, emphasis added)

But you have come to Mount Zion, to the heavenly Jerusalem, the city of the living God. You have come to thousands upon thousands of angels in joyful assembly, to the church of the firstborn, whose names are written in heaven. You have come to God, the judge of all men, to the spirits of righteous men made perfect [cf. the Old Testament saints listed in Heb 11], to Jesus the mediator of a new covenant, and to the sprinkled blood that speaks a better word than the blood of Abel. (Heb 12:22-24)

The text in Zephaniah, admittedly a rather obscure and little-known passage of Scripture, is actually a profound expression of the meaning of the gospel and the joy that we can experience as a result of that gospel.[43] In the light of its New Testament fulfillment in Christ, we can see that Zephaniah's call for the people of God to sing joyfully has been made possible by the cross of Christ that has taken away our punishment. The "good news" is that now God is *present* to us and not far away ("the LORD your God is with you"), that God is *powerful* and not powerless to help us ("mighty to save"), that he has *pleasure* in being near to his people ("great delight in you"), that he imparts his *peace* and soothing love to his people ("he will quiet you with his love"). The maternal imagery of a mother comforting and soothing her child is a

---

[43]I would like to thank the Rev. Mario Bergner for drawing this text to my attention several years ago. This is apparently the only text in the entire Bible in which God is portrayed as *singing*. Singing is a natural expression of inner joy and exultation, and from all eternity Father, Son and Holy Spirit have enjoyed exultation and joy in communion with one another. Accordingly, it is justifiable to think of an *eternal song* being sung in the heart of the Trinity, and the songs of God's people in worship are our response to and participation in the heavenly, trinitarian choir.

striking contrast to the masculine imagery of God as Lord, Judge and King. Zephaniah depicts the *grace* of God not in abstract terms ("the unmerited favor of God") but in the very concrete images of a parent who is delighted with her child and enjoying being close to the child.

In meditation we can pair Zephaniah's text with the writer of Hebrews' vision of the heavenly worship, where "heaven is a happy and joyful place," with God the Father and God the Son and the redeemed people of God enjoying being close to one another! The God of Zephaniah and the God of the writer of Hebrews is a God pleased and delighted with his people—and as we meditate on such texts and internalize them, they can help to reshape our images of God and deepen our loving communion with our Father.[44] Consider the following account of "G," a seminary student, of his meditation on Hebrews 12 and the heavenly worship:

> I found reflecting on the contrast between coming to Mount Sinai and to Mount Zion in Hebrews 12 to be overwhelming. . . . Whereas they had a terrifying experience at Sinai, my experience is like the joyous gathering at the heavenly Jerusalem amidst congregations and saints and angels singing praises. . . . I was led into a reflection on joy. . . . I have felt over-busy and pulled in many directions these past months. Meditating on this passage convicted me to return continually to communion with God and recognition of invisible reality so that I can act in joy. I now feel compelled to make it my goal to live my life as conscious, joyous worship in the presence of the saints and angels.

This student's meditative experience led to a deeper understanding of worship from a heavenly perspective and a deeper experience of joy in God.

As a third example, consider the pairing of Ephesians 1:3; 2:6; and 2 Corinthians 3:18, Pauline propositional statements, and Revelation 21–22, John's visionary description of the new Jerusalem:

---

[44]In a 2006 survey of American religious attitudes and beliefs, researchers at Baylor University found that many Americans, including evangelical Christians, had images of God in which anger was very prominent: "American Piety in the 21st Century: New Insights into the Depths and Complexity of Religion in the US," Baylor Institute for Studies of Religion, Waco, Tex., September 2006, p. 27, on the authoritarian and critical images of God. These studies suggest that many American Christians could be spiritually benefited by whole-brain meditation on sonship, adoption and the love of God.

> Praise be to the God and Father of our Lord Jesus Christ, who has blessed us in the heavenly realms with every spiritual blessing in Christ. (Eph 1:3)

> God raised us up with Christ and seated us with him in the heavenly realms in Christ Jesus. (Eph 2:6)

> We, who with unveiled faces all reflect the Lord's glory, are being transformed into his likeness with ever-increasing glory, which comes from the Lord, who is the Spirit. (2 Cor 3:18)

> I saw the Holy City, the new Jerusalem, coming out of heaven from God, prepared as a bride beautifully dressed for her husband. . . . It shone with the glory of God, and its brilliance was like that of a very precious jewel, like a jasper, clear as crystal. . . . He measured the city . . . and found it to be 1,400 miles in length, and as wide and high as it is long.
>
> They will see his face, and his name will be on their foreheads. . . . They will not need the light of a lamp or the light of the sun, for the Lord God will give them light. And they will reign for ever and ever. (Rev 21:2, 11, 16; 22:4-5)

Paul's statement that God the Father has blessed his redeemed children with *every* spiritual blessing in the heavenly places is a staggering assertion of the unimaginably great scope of the divine generosity in the gospel: every blessing that we could imagine, and then more, are ours in Christ, as we share in union with him the fullness of the Son's life with the Father in the communion of the Holy Spirit.

Paul's reference in Ephesians 1:3 to the "heavenly realms" may seem a bit thin and abstract, taken by itself; but read in the light of Revelation 21–22, it takes on vivid meaning. We are seated with Christ in the heavenly realms by virtue of our union with him, being connected to Christ by the Holy Spirit (1 Cor 12:13; 6:17). By virtue of the connecting bond of the Holy Spirit, our redeemed, extended self is lifted up to heaven and into the presence of Christ, where by faith and the Spirit, we behold with spiritual vision the glory of God in the face of Christ (2 Cor 3:18). This latter experience, true and available for all Christians ("we all reflect"), is the *already* of the beatific vision that will be fully consummated at the end.

Since we are truly seated with Christ, we can, by faith, see ourselves *inside* the new Jerusalem, into whose presence we have *already* come (Heb 12:22). The amazing magnitude of the new Jerusalem (a cube 1,400 miles on a side) is a fitting image of the staggering magnitude of the "every" blessing with which we have been blessed, and the images of jewels, gold and brilliant light are powerful images of the beauty, immensity and concentrated value and substantiality of the new creation compared to the present one. Spending much time meditating on the images of Revelation 21–22 is very much in keeping with Paul's apostolic command to focus the Christian consciousness and attention on the *things above*, where Christ is at the right hand of God (Col 3:1). Doing so renews the Christian imagination and recovers the sense of the transcendent beauty of the heavenly world and the Christian future that has largely disappeared from the modern church.

WORLDVIEW MEDITATION
THE FIVE PRACTICES OF RIGHT COMPREHENSION

The third and final method of biblical meditation to be discussed is a form of *worldview* meditation that I call the "Five Practices of Right Comprehension." This is a method of meditation that may have more appeal to those who are bit more inclined to theology in its systematic expressions, but I hope that every reader of this essay might at least give it a try. The purpose here is to encapsulate in five basic points or topics some essentials of a biblical and Christian worldview: our view of God, of reality or the world, of the self or the human person, of the basic purpose of human life, and the basic nature of worship.

These five points do not, of course, cover all the essential points of Christian faith, and the list could have been easily expanded to ten points or more, but it is my desire to keep this meditative exercise within practicable bounds and not to discourage a would-be practitioner with too daunting a task. The five points or practices that have been chosen are, in my judgment, points that particularly need some refocusing or recalibration in contemporary American evangelicalism. The value of such a worldview meditation is that it can provide a firm foundation for Christian discipleship and Bible study generally, by reminding us of the big picture within which we live our Christian lives and read our Bibles.

Here are the "Five Practices of Right Comprehension," with some suggested Scriptures for meditation on each point, and some explanation:

1. Right comprehension of God
The triune God, Father, Son and Holy Spirit

> May the grace of the Lord Jesus Christ, and the love of God [the Father], and the fellowship of the Holy Spirit be with you all. (2 Cor 13:14)

> He saw the Spirit of God descending like a dove and lighting on him. And a voice from heaven said, "This is my beloved Son, whom I love, with him I am well pleased." (Mt 3:16-17)

> While he was a long way off, his father saw him and was filled with compassion for him; he ran to his son, threw his arms around him and kissed him. (Lk 15:20)

This point reminds us that God is a Trinity of persons—Father, Son and Holy Spirit. American evangelicals can at times practice a unitarianism of the second person, so to speak, that neglects the Father and the Holy Spirit. We are reminded here that ultimate reality is found eternally not in matter but in spirit, and in a *community of persons in loving, committed relationships:* a good counterweight to the individualistic tendencies of our culture. The texts in Matthew and Luke help to put faces on the triune persons and can help to imprint the liberating images of a loving and compassionate Father on the Christian's heart and mind. This point of meditation reminds us that our Christian life is inherently about *good relationships* and not just about me or myself, and that our very salvation has a trinitarian basis: our participation in the Father's love for the Son, in the fellowship of the Holy Spirit.

2. Right comprehension of reality
The heavenly, unseen world

> Since, then, you have been raised with Christ, set your hearts on things above, where Christ is, at the right hand of God. (Col 3:1)

> So we fix our eyes not on what is seen, but on what is unseen. For what is seen is temporary, but what is unseen is eternal. (2 Cor 4:18)

Those who use the things of this world, [should live] as if not engrossed in them. For this world in its present form is passing away. (1 Cor 7:31)

I saw the Holy City, the new Jerusalem, coming down out of heaven from God, prepared as a bride beautifully dressed for her husband. . . . It shone with the glory of God, and its brilliance was like that of a very precious jewel, like a jasper, clear as crystal. . . . He measured the city . . . and found it to be 1,400 miles in length, and as wide and high as it is long. . . .

They will see his face, and his name will be on their foreheads. . . . They will not need the light of the sun, for the Lord God will give them light. And they will reign for ever and ever. (Rev 21:2, 11, 16; 22:4-5)

These texts are decidedly countercultural in that they challenge the predominantly *this-worldly* and *materialistic* mindsets reinforced by the cultures of science, technology and digital media. They remind us that the invisible things of heaven are not only real but in the last analysis, more lasting and important than the material forces and objects that we think we can manipulate and control. This material world is real and good as God's creation, but it is not eternal, and we look to the future when God will transform it and replace it with an environment that is unimaginably more beautiful and satisfying. Letting our minds linger over the images of the heavenly Jerusalem can provide some much-needed emotional and intellectual distance from the materialism and consumerism of our culture.

3. Right comprehension of self
The trinitarian-ecclesial self

If anyone is in Christ, he is a new creation. (2 Cor 5:17)

I have been crucified with Christ and it is no longer I who live, but Christ lives in me. (Gal 2:20)

We were all baptized by one Spirit into one body—whether Jews or Greeks, slave or free—and we were all given the one Spirit to drink. (1 Cor 12:13)

This third point, the "right comprehension of self," is a crucial one for American Christians, or modern Christians generally, because it challenges in the most fundamental way the individualism of Western culture.

As Christians, our fundamental identity is not a matter of ethnic or national origin, social class or gender, but rather that of a *trinitarian-ecclesial self:* from the time of our conversion and our incorporation into the body of Christ by the Holy Spirit, our fundamental identity is based on our real, lasting relationships with the persons of the Trinity and with the members of the body of Christ. Our old, autonomous, individualistic identities are dead, nailed to the cross; our true identity is *in Christ* and *with the body.* We do ministry not as autonomous lone rangers but the way that the triune God does ministry: in partnership, consultation and cooperation with the other members of the church, the body of Christ. We need to constantly remind ourselves, *This is who I really am—not an autonomous individual, but one united to Christ and to the fellow members of his body.*

4. Right comprehension of purpose
To glorify God and to enjoy him forever

> In him we were also chosen . . . in order that we, who were the first to hope in Christ, might be for the praise of his glory. . . . [We] were marked in him . . . until the redemption of those who are God's possession—to the praise of his glory. (Eph 1:11-12, 14)

> Bring my sons from afar
>> and my daughters from the ends of the earth—
>> everyone who is called by my name,
>> whom I created for my glory,
>> whom I formed and made. (Is 43:6-7)

> You will fill me with joy in your presence,
> with eternal pleasures at your right hand. (Ps 16:11)

> At that time Jesus, full of joy through the Holy Spirit, said, "I praise you Father, Lord of heaven and earth." (Lk 10:21)

These texts are consistent with the classic answer to the Question 1 in the Westminster Shorter Catechism: "What is the chief end [purpose] of man? Man's chief end is to glorify God and to enjoy him forever." We glorify God as we love him, obey his commands, and render him praise, adoration and thanksgiving in private and especially corporate worship. Worship, insofar as it involves being in the presence of the God who loves us, is the highest act of the human being and can be life's most enjoyable and satisfying experience. To be in God's presence as a redeemed child of God is to experience joy. The text in Luke 10, with its tiny vignette of Jesus' experience of joy in the Holy Spirit as he gives praise to the Father, is a beautiful picture on earth of the eternal dynamics of the Trinity, who experience the deepest joy in their mutual praising and giving honor to one another. Our worship on earth, in the Spirit, is a real participation in the heavenly worship above, where we are truly present to God, as the fifth point reminds us: Since we are united to Christ by the Spirit, the picture of Jesus' joy in praising the Father (Lk 10:21) can become a beautiful picture of our own experience in worship, as we in fact worship in the presence of heaven itself (Heb 10:22-25).

5. Right comprehension of worship
The holy God who is really present

> In the year that King Uzziah died, I saw the Lord seated on a throne, high and exalted, and the train of his robe filled the temple. Above him were seraphs. . . . And they were calling to one another:
>
> > "Holy, holy, holy is the LORD Almighty;
> > the whole earth is full of his glory." (Is 6:1-3)
>
> When you are assembled in the name of the Lord Jesus . . . and the power of our Lord Jesus is present . . . (1 Cor 5:4)
>
> He will fall down and worship God, exclaiming, "God is really among you!" (1 Cor 14:25)
>
> You have come to Mount Zion, to the heavenly Jerusalem, the city of the living God. You have come to thousands upon thousands of angels in joyful assembly, to the church of the firstborn, whose names are written in heaven. You have come to God, the judge of all men, to the spirits of righteous men made perfect, to Jesus the mediator of a new covenant, and to the sprinkled blood that speaks a better word than the blood of Abel. (Heb 12:22-24)

It has been said that much of modern worship runs the risk of being, in practice, unitarian, deistic and Pelagian—meaning, focusing on Jesus only, rather than being conscious of all three persons of the

Trinity; deistic in the sense of God seeming far away, not near to his people and truly present in the midst of the assembly; and Pelagian in the sense of being a human performance accomplished on human power and energy. These texts remind us that God is *really present* in the midst of his people, that worship involves the presence of not merely human energy but rather the supernatural energy of the Holy Spirit, that heaven is not just "up there" or only in the future, but in our midst and "already."

The "name of Jesus" is not just a personal tag or identifying mark, but the risen Lord's extended self, by which he is personally, powerfully and actively present. The "name" is like Christ's own wireless hotspot in the midst of the assembly through which he projects his power and presence to us as his church below. The risen Christ, who stands at the door of our churches and waits to be acknowledged and invited in (Rev 3:20), is not only the (passive) recipient of worship but the *active* and *primary* subject and actor in worship, who speaks to his people in Word and sacrament and who enjoys table fellowship with them.

This fifth point in the "Five Practices of Right Comprehension" is a good summation and corporate expression of the first four, and leads us in a natural movement of thought back to the right comprehension of God, the blessed Trinity, Father, Son and Holy Spirit, God blessed forever.

The five practices can be meditated on as a group for perhaps a period of thirty minutes or so, ideally on a weekly basis, to reinforce our Christian worldview. There are no rigid rules here, of course; spending as much or little time on one or more points as the Spirit leads may be quite beneficial as well.

CONCLUDING UNSCIENTIFIC POSTSCRIPT
Student Testimonies on Meditation

This chapter ends with some personal testimonies by seminary students on their own experiences with biblical meditation on various biblical texts. These testimonies speak for themselves and, I hope, will encourage you to begin or to continue this most valuable and ancient spiritual practice:

Jesus' High Priestly Prayer (Jn 17:20-26)

Although it was somewhat difficult to concentrate on a single passage for a long duration of time, particularly in the midst of the busyness of academics, I was really blessed by this opportunity to meditate on Jesus' High Priestly Prayer. . . . As I meditated . . . I was incredibly moved and warmed by how much Jesus cares and expresses concern for us; that it is not simply out of obedience, but also out of genuine love . . . as a Savior who thirsts and hungers for his people to be united with him and to be made complete and ultimately, to know the divine love that alone brings true fulfillment. (D. C.)

The vine and the branches: Abiding in Jesus (Jn 15:1-17)

This has been hugely formative! First, the meditation helped me slow down enough to "notice" the Holy Spirit illuminating and applying certain aspects of the texts. Second, the theme of "Abiding in Jesus" has been the thread throughout the whole term. I am continually asking, "Does this help me abide . . . ?" My morning devotions usually have so much content that it never gets this deep or formative. (S. F.)

Through this interaction with the Scripture, I was able to retreat from the daily grind of work and school. . . . Through this prayerful reflection on the text, I had an epiphany of what it means to be bound to Christ. . . . I have found renewed confidence in the grace and steadfast connection to Christ through his redeeming power. . . . This passage is so packed with insight . . . that I continue to attempt to unpack everything that is being said here. (J. M.)

Life in the Spirit (Rom 8:1-17)

The exercise was a challenging one. It was difficult to "simply" contemplate the text and avoid more intellectual and academic approaches to the text. I was saddened to realize how little I knew how to contemplate, when at one point this had been my primary way of reading Scripture. . . . One day in particular, I felt especially drawn toward God's presence. . . . It was special to feel God inviting me into His presence, whereas I often feel compelled to conjure up or force my mind to postulate God's presence. For one day, it felt natural. . . . It was a good exercise and one I need more practice at. (M. H.)

Every day, early in the morning . . . I read this passage and memorized it. . . . On April 4th or 5th I was surprised that the Word was speaking to me from the inside of my heart. . . . At some moments, I could know that God was with me. . . . I felt that Hands were holding my shoulders from behind, when I prayed. (J. T.)

Christ the Good Shepherd (Jn 10:1-18)

I really enjoyed this exercise. . . . If anything, this helped my concentration. This was a way of meditation and reflection that filled my soul as a result of slow, repeated reading. Focusing on Christ as the Door was a new concept to me—I've never really focused on that passage before. (E. B.)

The Five Practices of Right Comprehension

I enjoyed this assignment and would encourage you to continue to use it in class. . . . Seminary is so busy that it is easy to find excuses not to sit down and pray. . . . The Five Practices offered me a new way of reading and meditating on Scripture. . . . Bringing an overarching theme for reflection is something I had done before . . . but not so intentionally. . . . Such specific instruction in prayer is probably rare in 21st-century American evangelical circles. . . . Thank you for introducing me to the Five Practices, and I affirm the value of this method of meditation. (G. Z.)

We found that the Five Practices were tremendously helpful. Logistically, the instructions could have been slightly clearer. However, the experience itself was awesome. . . . We all felt both inward toward joy in God and outward toward inviting others to share that divine joy and approval. (J. S., J. T., J. S. and G. Z.)

* * * * *

Oh, how I love your law!
I meditate on it all day long. (Ps 119:97)

Blessed is the one
who does not walk in step with the wicked. . . .
but whose delight is in the law of the LORD,
and who meditates on his law day and night. (Ps 1:1-2 NIV 2011)

Acknowledgments

Typically, a book is the result of the labors and insights of many, and this one is no exception. I wish to give special thanks to Gary Deddo, David Congdon, Allison Rieck and their editorial staff at IVP Academic for their careful and attentive work on this manuscript. Special thanks also go to my wife, Robin, for her careful reading of the galley proofs.

My colleagues Gwenfair Adams, Sam Schutz, Steve Kang, Susan Currie, Sean McDonough, Steve Klipowicz, Beth Maynard, and my students in Systematic Theology III gave helpful suggestions and feedback along the way. Any deficiencies in matters of fact or interpretation are, of course, due to the author alone.

John Jefferson Davis
Gordon-Conwell Theological Seminary
S. Hamilton, Massachusetts

Select Bibliography

Books

Austin, James H. *Zen and the Brain: Toward an Understanding of Meditation and Consciousness*. Cambridge, Mass.: MIT Press, 1998.

Barcley, William B. *"Christ in You": A Study in Paul's Theology and Ethics*. Lanham, Md.: University Press of America, 1999.

Beale, G. K. *The Temple and the Church's Mission: A Biblical Theology of the Dwelling Place of God*. Downers Grove, Ill.: InterVarsity Press, 2004.

Benson, Herbert. *The Relaxation Response*. New York: Avon Books, 1975.

Bianchi, Enzo. *Praying the Word: An Introduction to Lectio Divina*. Kalamazoo, Mich.: Cistercian Studies, 1999.

Carr, Nicholas. *The Shallows: What the Internet Is Doing to Our Brains*. New York: W. W. Norton, 2010.

Casey, Michael. *Sacred Reading: The Ancient Art of Lectio Divina*. Liguori, Mo.: Triumph Books, 1996.

Chan, Simon. *Spiritual Theology: A Systematic Study of the Christian Life*. Downers Grove, Ill.: InterVarsity Press, 1998.

Clowney, Edmund. *CM: Christian Meditation*. Nutley, N.J.: Craig, 1979.

Conyers, A. J. *The Loss of Transcendence and Its Effects on Modern Life*. South Bend, Ind.: St. Augustine's, 1999.

Csikszentmihaly, Mihaly. *Flow: The Psychology of Optimal Experience*. New York: HarperCollins, 1990.

Eck, Diana L. *A New Religious America: How a 'Christian' Country Has Become the World's Most Religiously Diverse Nation*. New York: Harper-Collins, 2001.

Fairbairn, Donald. *Life in the Trinity: An Introduction to Theology with the Help of the Church Fathers*. Downers Grove, Ill.: IVP Academic, 2009.

Foster, Richard J. *Celebration of Discipline: The Path to Spiritual Growth*. New York: Harper and Row, 1978.

Goleman, Daniel. *The Meditative Mind: The Varieties of Meditative Experience*. Los Angeles: Jeremy P. Tarcher, 1988.

Hall, Thelma. *Too Deep for Words*. Mahwah, N.J.: Paulist, 1988.

Hawkins, Greg L., and Parkinson, Cally. *Reveal: Where Are You? The Brutal Truth About Spiritual Growth*. Barrington, Ill.: Willow Creek Association, 2007.

Honore, Carl. *In Praise of Slow: How a Worldwide Movement Is Challenging the Cult of Speed*. Toronto: Alfred A. Knopf, 2004.

Howard, Evan. *Praying the Scriptures*. Downers Grove, Ill.: InterVarsity Press, 1999.

Keating, Thomas. *Intimacy with God*. New York: Crossroad, 1994.

Lossky, Vladimir. *The Mystical Theology of the Eastern Church*. Crestwood, N.Y.: St. Vladimir's Seminary Press, 1993.

Lubac, Henri de. *Medieval Exegesis*, vol. 4. Translated by Mark Sebanc. Grand Rapids: Eerdmans, 1998.

Magrassi, Mariono. *Praying the Bible: An Introduction to Lectio Divina*. Collegeville, Minn.: Liturgical, 1998.

Mayer, Richard E. *Multi-Media Learning*, 2nd ed. New York: Cambridge University Press, 2009.

Miedema, John. *Slow Reading*. Duluth, Minn.: Litwin Books, 2009.

Muto, Susan. *A Practical Guide to Spiritual Reading*. Danville, N.J.: Dimension Books, 1976.

Newberg, Andrew, and Mark Robert Waldman. *How God Changes Your Brain*. New York: Ballantine Books, 2009.

O'Keefe, John J., and R. R Reno. *Sanctified Vision: An Introduction to Early Christian Interpretation*. Baltimore: Johns Hopkins University Press, 2005.

Pennington, Basil. *Lectio Divina: Renewing the Ancient Practice of Praying the Scriptures*. New York: Crossroad, 1998.

Piper, John. *Desiring God: Meditations of a Christian Hedonist*. Sisters, Ore.: Multnomah Books, 1996.

Scazzero, Peter. *Emotionally Healthy Spirituality*. Nashville: Thomas Nelson, 2006.

Sider, Ronald J. *The Scandal of the Evangelical Conscience: Why Are Christians Living Just Like the Rest of the World?* Grand Rapids: Baker Books, 2005.

Thompson, Curt. *Anatomy of the Soul: Surprising Connections Between Neuroscience and Spiritual Practices That Can Transform Your Life and Relationships*. Carrollton, Tex.: SaltRiver/Tyndale House, 2010.

Toon, Peter. *The Art of Meditating on Scripture*. Grand Rapids: Zondervan, 1993.

Torrance, James B. *Worship, Community & the Triune God of Grace*. Downers Grove, Ill.: InterVarsity Press, 1996.

Tunink, Wilfrid. *Vision of Peace: A Study of Benedictine Monastic Life.* New York: Farrar, Straus, 1963.

Underhill, Evelyn. *Mysticism.* London: Methuen, 1930; 1962.

Vitz, Paul C. *Psychology as Religion: The Cult of Self-Worship.* Grand Rapids: Eerdmans, 1977.

Wikenhauser, Alfred. *Pauline Mysticism: Christ in the Mystical Teaching of St. Paul.* Edinburgh-London: Nelson, 1960.

Willard, Dallas. *The Spirit of the Disciplines: Understanding How God Changes Lives.* New York: HarperCollins, 1988.

Zengotita, Thomas de. *Mediated: How the Media Shapes Your World and the Way You Live in It.* New York: Bloomsbury, 2005.

Zizioulas, John. *Being as Communion: Studies in Personhood and the Church.* Crestwood, N.Y.: St. Vladimir's Seminary Press, 1993.

Articles

Allen, Thomas G. "Exaltation and Solidarity with Christ: Ephesians 1:20 and 2:6." *Journal for the Study of the New Testament* 28 (1986): 103-20.

Beeke, Joel. "The Puritan Practice of Meditation." www.banneroftruth.org/pages/articles_detail.php?119.

Clark, Andy, and David J. Chalmers. "The Extended Mind." *Analysis* 58 (1998): 10-23.

Dupre, Louis. "The Christian Experience of Mystical Union." *Journal of Religion* 69 (1989): 1-13.

Fairbairn, Donald. "Patristic Exegesis and Theology: The Cart and the Horse." *Westminster Theological Journal* 69 (2007): 1-19.

Jones, R. Tudor. "Union with Christ: The Existential Nerve of Puritan Piety." *Tyndale Bulletin* 41, no. 2 (1990): 186-208.

Kaiser, Walter C., Jr. "What Is Biblical Meditation?" pp. 39-53. In *Renewing Your Mind in a Secular World,* edited by John D. Woodbridge. Chicago: Moody Press, 1985.

Kline, Meredith G. "Space and Time in the Genesis Cosmogony." *Perspectives on Science and Christian Faith* 48 (1996): 2-15.

Lutz, Antoine, John D. Dunne and Richard J. Davidson. "Meditation and the Neuro-Science of Consciousness: An Introduction," pp. 499-551. In *The Cambridge Handbook of Consciousness,* edited by Philip David Zelazo et al. Cambridge: Cambridge University Press, 2007.

Nauss, Allen. "Preaching Sermons That Will Be Remembered." *Concordia Journal* 34, no. 4 (October 2008): 264-91.

Ratzinger, Joseph Cardinal. "Letter to the Bishops of the Catholic Church on Some Aspects of Christian Meditation," Congregation of the Doctrine of the Faith, October 15, 1989. www.ewtn.com/library/curia/cdfmed.htm.

Scorgie, Glen. "Hermeneutics and the Meditative Use of Scripture: the Case for a Baptized Imagination." www.bethel.edu/~gscorgie/articles/hermeneutics.

Steinmetz, David C. "The Superiority of Pre-Critical Exegesis." *Theology Today* 37, no. 1 (April 1980): 27-38.

Name and Subject Index

Scripture Index